This book is presented to

_____

It was given to you by

_____

Date

_____

Based on the Classic Devotional by Oswald Chambers
My Utmost for His Highest

Jesus Wants All of Me

Bedtime Prayer
Edition

Approved by the Oswald Chambers Publications Association
Adapted and Illustrated by Phil A. Smouse

BARBOUR
PUBLISHING

ISBN 978-1-59789-675-7

This book is based upon *My Utmost for His Highest* by Oswald Chambers. Original edition © 1935 by Dodd, Mead & Company, Inc., © renewed 1963 by the Oswald Chambers Publications Assn., Ltd., and published by special arrangement with and permission of the Oswald Chambers Publications Association, Ltd., and Discovery House Publishers, 3000 Kraft Avenue SE, Grand Rapids, Michigan 49512.

Cover artist: Phil A. Smouse

Scripture quotations are taken from the New King James Version®. Copyright © 1982 by Thomas Nelson, Inc. Used by permission. All rights reserved.

Published by Barbour Publishing, Inc., P.O. Box 719, Uhrichsville, Ohio 44683, www.barbourbooks.com

Our mission is to publish and distribute inspirational products offering exceptional value and biblical encouragement to the masses.

 Member of the
Evangelical Christian
Publishers Association

Printed in Malaysia.

For Maurice
and for "purity of motive."

To the Parent

Oswald Chambers understood the secret of the Christian life—that he must give himself completely to God. And because he did, God has used Oswald Chambers's book *My Utmost for His Highest* to draw millions of readers into a deeper relationship with Himself.

Jesus wants the very same from each of us. He wants us to be His—100 percent. And the most important thing is not what we say or do, or even who we reach. The most important thing is the relationship we cultivate with Him.

That deep spiritual connection isn't only for adults. In fact, Jesus Himself talked about having a childlike faith.

And just as it is impossible for a young child to draw a bad picture, I believe with all my heart it is impossible for a little heart to pray a bad prayer.

But where do you begin?

Based on Chambers's classic devotional and personal prayer journal, *Jesus Wants All of Me: Bedtime Prayer Edition* can be your guide as a parent to help your children develop a deeper relationship with God.

These daily thoughts and prayers will teach your children truths from God's Word that will stay with them the rest of their lives—and put the sound of a heart pouring itself out to Jesus in their ears and on their lips—so time spent with Him will become as natural *and necessary* as breathing.

What could be more important than that? Use this devotional to help your children meet—and give their hearts to—Jesus.

Phil A. Smouse

Jesus Wants All of Me

January 1

I am God's.
My heart
is His heart.
My mind
is His mind.
My eyes will
look for Him.
My ears will listen for
His voice. My hands will
do His will. *I am God's!*

Now also Christ will be magnified in my body.
PHILIPPIANS 1:20

A Prayer

O Jesus, here is my heart. Please forgive me for taking so long to wake up and see just how much You really love me. I want to see You face-to-face.

My thoughts for Jesus

_____

_____

Where Are We Going?

January 2

God knows
what will
happen
tomorrow.
He knows
where I will be. He
knows what I will do.
I don't have to worry.
I am in good hands.
I am in God's hands!

*He went out,
not knowing
where he
was going.*
HEBREWS 11:8

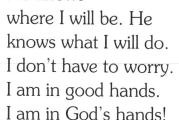

A Prayer

Jesus, I want to know You. Not in a small,
Sunday morning way, but in a way that is as
big and amazing and everlasting as You are.

My thoughts for Jesus

_____

_____

I Can See Clearly Now

January 3

I can talk to God. And God can talk to me! God speaks to me from His Word. His Word is the Bible. God's Spirit inside of me will help me understand what the Bible says. When God speaks, I will listen.

Clouds and darkness surround Him.
PSALM 97:2

A Prayer

O Lord, speak to my heart. I want to know Your voice. Please blow away the clouds that hide Your face so I can see the light of Your great love.

My thoughts for Jesus

_____

_____

Wait for Me!

January 4

God answers my
prayers. At times
He says, "Yes."
Other times He
says, "No." And every
now and then God will say,
"Wait." I don't like to wait.
But if God says, "Wait,"
I will wait. I won't run
ahead of Him. I will follow.

*"Lord, why
can I not
follow
You now?"*
JOHN 13:37

A Prayer

Jesus, fill my heart to bursting so that the words
I speak and the things I do will shine with the
beautiful, blazing light of Your love.

My thoughts for Jesus

_____

_____

Follow the Leader

January 5

I will follow
Jesus. I don't
have to make
promises to Him.
I know I won't
always understand.
I don't need to be perfect.
I only need to follow Him.
Jesus loves me.

*"You shall
follow Me
afterward."*
JOHN 13:36

A Prayer

O Lord, here is my heart. I am Yours to mold and
make as You desire. Please take my life and make
it everything You ever wanted it to be.

My thoughts for Jesus

_____

_____

Give It Back!

January 6

What is the very best thing God has ever given to me? God wants me to give it back! He wants me to share that gift with someone else. That's why He gave it to me. I won't keep God's gift to myself. I will give it back!

There he built an altar to the Lord.
GENESIS 12:8

A Prayer

Thank You, Jesus, for all the good things You've given me. Teach me not to hold them too tightly. You are my one true love. I want to be like You.

My thoughts for Jesus

_____

_____

Do I Know Him?

January 7

When I like someone, I want to spend time with that person. We do things together. That's what makes us friends. I want to spend time with God. I want to be best friends with Him.

"Have I been with you so long, and yet you have not known Me?"
JOHN 14:9

A Prayer

O Jesus, I love You so much. Please let me be a delight to Your heart and a breath of pure joy to everyone I meet today.

My thoughts for Jesus

_____

_____

I Give Up

January 8

God wants
all of me.
He wants
me to give
Him every-
thing. Whatever
I do, He wants me
to be thinking about
Him. God loves me!

*And Abraham
built an altar. . .
and bound Isaac
his son.*
GENESIS 22:9

A Prayer

Thank You, Jesus, for allowing me to serve You in a
way that pleases You. I am ready to be Your hands
and feet in each and every moment of this new day.

My thoughts for Jesus

_____

_____

So Big!

January 9

God made
the morning and the evening.
He made the mighty mountains.
He made the oceans and everything in them. But God is brighter
than the morning. He is higher
than the mountains. His love for
me is deeper than any ocean.
God made me. And He will
make me be like His Son.
He will make me be like Jesus.

*May your
whole
spirit,
soul,
and
body be
preserved
blameless.*
1 THESSALONIANS
5:23

A Prayer

O Lord, draw me close to Your heart today. Please
take away these sins You know so well. And shine
Your holy light on the ones I can't seem to see.

My thoughts for Jesus

_____

_____

For Me?

January 10

Jesus will give me a beautiful gift. He will take all my sins away. But how do I get His gift? Do I promise to be good? What do I have to do? I don't have to do anything! I just have to open my heart to Jesus.

"Open their eyes . . .that they may receive."
Acts 26:18

A Prayer

Thank You, Lord, for more! More kindness and gentleness. More longing to do Your will. More patience with people and things. And most of all, more of You.

My thoughts for Jesus

_____

_____

Grumpy, Grumpy

January 11

Sometimes, when I obey the Bible, other people will feel upset. But God wants me to obey Him no matter what other people say or do. I don't like it when others are upset. But God will care for them. And I will let Him.

. . .and on [Simon] they laid the cross.
LUKE 23:26

A Prayer

Lord, let everything I say and do give praise to You. Please keep my heart in tune with Yours so that others may find and know Your beauty and joy.

My thoughts for Jesus

_____

_____

He Knows My Name

January 12

Why do I feel this way? Why can't I understand myself? I just don't know. But Jesus knows. He knows even when I don't. Maybe something is wrong. Maybe I need to change. I will let Jesus change my heart.

When they were alone, He explained all things to His disciples. MARK 4:34

A Prayer

O Jesus, thank You for this new day and for the courage to make a brand-new start. Please come inside and change my heart. I want to be like You.

My thoughts for Jesus

_____

_____

Quiet, Please!

January 13

Sometimes
I don't like
to be alone.
I feel lonely.
But when I'm
alone, everything
is quiet. I can talk to God.
If I listen, maybe I'll hear
Him answer me.

*When He
was alone. . .
the twelve
asked Him.*
MARK 4:10

A Prayer

This is the day the Lord has made. Let my eyes
and my ears and my heart and my mind be Yours
and Yours alone today.

My thoughts for Jesus

_____

_____

Called by God

January 14

People need to
know about God's
love. And God wants
them to know. Someone should
probably tell them! But who
should it be? Whom has God
picked? He has picked someone
very special. He has picked me.
He wants me to tell people that
God loves them.

*Then I said,
"Here am I!
Send me."*
ISAIAH 6:8

A Prayer

O Lord, You are good. Thank You for Your loving
kindness and for working in all things and every
way for my good today. I love You.

My thoughts for Jesus

_____

_____

Out with the Old

January 15

I am born
again. God
took the dirty,
stinky things
in me and
buried them.
They are gone! I won't dig
them up. I don't want them
back. God's love makes me
new and clean.

*We also
should walk
in newness
of life.*
Romans 6:4

A Prayer

Lord, thank You for Your Word. You alone are God.
And You are holy. Breathe the breath of new life
into my heart this day. I want to be like You.

My thoughts for Jesus

_____

_____

It's for You

January 16

God is calling me. He has a job for me to do! What great thing should I do for Him? I know! I will get down on my knees. I will listen for His voice. I will find out what He wants. Then I will get up and do it.

I heard the voice of the Lord, saying: "Whom shall I send?"
ISAIAH 6:8

A Prayer

Jesus, here is my heart. I want to know You. Make me quiet on the inside so I can hear Your voice today.

My thoughts for Jesus

_____

_____

Okay, I'm Coming!

January 17

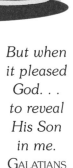

God is calling me. He has a wonderful plan for my life. And I will do amazing things. But God wants me to *be* something much more than He wants me to *do* something. He wants me to be like His Son.

But when it pleased God. . . to reveal His Son in me.
GALATIANS 1:15–16

A Prayer

"My Father will honor the one who serves me." Lord, I hear Your voice and I am coming. Take my life and make me Your servant today.

My thoughts for Jesus

_____

_____

That's Good!

January 18

I can do many
good things for
other people.
I can help.
I can listen.
I can be a friend. I love
to do good things. But
I love God more than
anything else.

*Thomas
answered and
said to Him,
"My Lord and
my God!"*
JOHN 20:28

A Prayer

O Lord, every good thing I have comes from You.
Let me show others the same kindness, gentleness, patience, and love that You have shown me.

My thoughts for Jesus

_____

_____

Darkness

January 19

Sometimes I just don't understand. I feel like I'm all alone in the dark. Where is God? I can't find Him. I can't reach Him. I am so small, and He is so

Great darkness fell upon him.
GENESIS 15:12

far away. But if I wait, God will show me that He is here with me. Maybe not right away, but He will show me. And when He does, I will see again. I will see His face. God is real.

A Prayer

Jesus, I want to know You. But my sins are pushing You away. Please take away the darkness that fills my heart and flood me with the light of Your love.

My thoughts for Jesus

_____

_____

Ready for Everything

January 20

I am born again. Jesus made everything new. I can do fun things. I can do difficult things. And I can enjoy them both. God's love is alive in my heart. When I'm close to God, I never feel bored.

"Unless one is born again, he cannot see the kingdom of God." JOHN 3:3

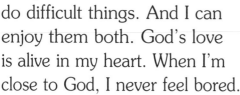

A Prayer

Jesus, I am lost without You. Breathe the breath of Your new life into me so my heart and my mind and all I say and do will be pleasing in Your sight.

My thoughts for Jesus

_____

_____

Now I Remember

January 21

Sometimes I forget that Jesus loves me. But He shows me His love in a thousand ways. Then I am so glad that He loves me. And, oh, how I love Him.

"I remember you, the kindness of your youth."
JEREMIAH 2:2

A Prayer

Jesus, how I long to see You face-to-face. My heart is so thirsty. Please come and touch me with Your love and kindness today. I want to be like You.

My thoughts for Jesus

_____

_____

Looking Up

January 22

Lord, You've given me so much—so much that I can't even see You anymore! Maybe I should stop looking at all the good things You've given me. Maybe I should set all this stuff aside and just start looking for You.

"Look to Me, and be saved."
ISAIAH 45:22

A Prayer

Jesus, thank You for changing my heart. Without Your new life there would be nothing good in me. You are all I really need. And I am looking to You.

My thoughts for Jesus

_____

_____

Mirror, Mirror

January 23

When people look at me, what do they see? Do they see Jesus? I will take time to be with Him.  When I spend more time with Jesus, I'll learn to act more like Him. I want to be like Jesus.

We. . .are being transformed into the same image.
2 CORINTHIANS 3:18

A Prayer

O Lord, please help me. I don't know what to do. Without Your love I'm no good for anything. Let me see Your beautiful face. I want to look just like You.

My thoughts for Jesus

_____

_____

Take It Personally

January 24

I know about Jesus. I know that He died on the cross. I know that He rose again. I know that He washed my sins away. But I don't want to just know about Jesus. I want to be friends with Him. I want to *know* Him.

"I have appeared to you for this purpose."
ACTS 26:16

A Prayer

Lord, bind my heart to Yours with the chains of Your great love. Surround me with Your mighty arms. I want to follow You wherever You may go.

My thoughts for Jesus

_____

_____

Surprise!

January 25

God will answer my prayers. But not always the way I expect Him to! He may surprise me. He may not! Who knows what God will do? But God will answer my prayers. I know He will!

But when it pleased God. . .
GALATIANS 1:15

A Prayer

Jesus, here is my heart. Please teach me how to trust You without being afraid. Take my life and knit it together with Yours until we both are one.

My thoughts for Jesus

_____

_____

It's That Simple

January 26

God has
my heart.
He will take
care of me.
I will always
have everything
I need. It's just that
simple. Thank You, Lord.

"Will He not much more clothe you?"
MATTHEW 6:30

A Prayer

O Lord, You are God alone. There is no other. You made the heavens and the earth. You know me by name. I am Your child. And I can call You "Daddy."

My thoughts for Jesus

_____

_____

I Never Thought about It

January 27

What will I eat?
What will I drink?
What will I wear?
And where will
it all come from?
I don't know. I never really
thought about it. Anyway,
Jesus told me not to worry
about all that. He said He
would take care of it.

*"Do not worry
about your life."*
MATTHEW 6:25

A Prayer

Lord, I want to be with You in the secret place.
Hide me from the things that would pull us apart
and sweep me into Your presence, mighty King.

My thoughts for Jesus

_____

_____

My Way

January 28

I did it *my way*. I thought of everything by myself. I did all the work. I didn't ask anyone for help. *And I was wrong!* O Lord, I'm so sorry. I should have done it Your way.

"Saul, Saul, why are you persecuting Me?"
ACTS 26:14

A Prayer

Thank You, Jesus, for the peace that fills this day. And thank You for loving me and making me one with You just as You and the Father are one.

My thoughts for Jesus

_____

_____

His Way

January 29

O Lord,
I've made
such a mess
of things.
Everyone
is angry.
Everything is ruined. My way
doesn't work. I don't want my
way anymore. Please show me
Your way.

*"Who are
You, Lord?"*
ACTS 26:15

A Prayer

Jesus, let the beauty of Your awesome voice be
heard in this place today. Sing the song of Your
mighty power and love into my listening heart.

My thoughts for Jesus

_____

_____

Who Said That?

January 30

I will pray. God will show me what to do. I know His voice. I hear

Him in my heart. I see Him all around me. He will speak to me. And when He does, I will listen.

And Samuel was afraid to tell Eli the vision.
1 SAMUEL 3:15

A Prayer

Thank You, Lord Jesus, for the wonderful surprise of unexpected things. You are absolutely amazing. I love You more than anything.

My thoughts for Jesus

_____

_____

Too Good to Be True

January 31

Oh, I can be good! I can look good. I can sound good. I can do good things. And that's good! But God doesn't care how good I act on the outside. He wants me to know Jesus on the inside.

. . .separated to the gospel of God.
ROMANS 1:1

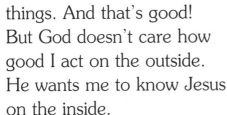

A Prayer

Jesus, please forgive me. I am so slow to thank You for all the good things You've done. Let me love You as deeply and recklessly as You love me.

My thoughts for Jesus

_____

_____

Your Love

February 1

People hurt me sometimes. Things go wrong. But that's all right. Jesus will heal the people who hurt me. He will fix the messed-up things. O Lord, here is my heart. Please let me tell someone about Your love.

For Christ did not send me to baptize, but to preach the gospel.
1 CORINTHIANS 1:17

A Prayer

O Lord, when I open my mouth to speak, let it be Your voice my friends hear and Your face they long to see. Let them be drawn to You and not to me.

My thoughts for Jesus

_____

_____

Who Cares?

February 2

Who cares about those people? Who cares if he knows Jesus? Who cares if she hears the Word of God? Who cares if someone tells him about God's love? Who cares if she finds God? Jesus cares. And so do I!

Woe is me if I do not preach the gospel!
1 CORINTHIANS 9:16

A Prayer

Jesus, without You there is only darkness. Please let the light of Your Holy Spirit rise like the morning sun and shine into every corner of this new day.

My thoughts for Jesus

_____

_____

Bad People
February 3

I can't love them! They've done too many bad things! But Jesus loves even people who do bad things. They are His children. I've done bad things, too, but Jesus made me good. I will tell them that Jesus loves them.

We have been made as the filth of the world.
1 CORINTHIANS 4:13

A Prayer

Jesus, I am Yours and Yours alone. Come and search my heart with the light of Your Word and take away everything that is not pleasing to You.

My thoughts for Jesus

_____

_____

Training Wheels

February 4

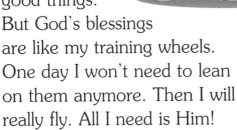

God does
so much for
me. He gives
me so many
good things.
But God's blessings
are like my training wheels.
One day I won't need to lean
on them anymore. Then I will
really fly. All I need is Him!

*For the love
of Christ
compels us.*
2 CORINTHIANS 5:14

A Prayer

Jesus, here is my heart. Please take the banged
up, broken down, rusted out, dirty, rough edges of
my life and make them into something beautiful.

My thoughts for Jesus

_____

_____

Here Am I
February 5

No one may ever know about the good things I do. No one

may ever hear about me. That's okay. I don't want to be famous. I don't need to be important. Jesus loves me. I will follow Him.

I am being poured out as a drink offering.
PHILIPPIANS 2:17

A Prayer

Thank You, Jesus, for this new day. Lead me on the path to Your secret place and I will run to meet You there.

My thoughts for Jesus

Here Is My Heart
February 6

Jesus, here is my heart. Please take away anything that makes You sad. I know it will hurt. But I will try not to cry. You will help me. You are everything that I ever dreamed You would be.

For I am already being poured out. . . .
2 TIMOTHY 4:6

A Prayer
O Lord, I have such a hard time being loving and kind to the people closest to me. Please come and change my heart. I want to be more like You.

My thoughts for Jesus

_____

_____

Are We There Yet?

February 7

I am so upset! I prayed and prayed. Why is God taking so long to answer? Didn't He hear me? Doesn't He care? Maybe I shouldn't be so worried about His answer. Maybe I should just get closer to Him.

"Besides all this, today is the third day."
LUKE 24:21

A Prayer

O Lord, I have so much to do. Please help me be still on the inside and know that You are God no matter what happens today.

My thoughts for Jesus

_____

_____

Just Like You

February 8

Jesus, I want
to be just like
You. I want
to see what
You see. I want
to feel what You
feel. Come into my heart.
Make my heart Your home.
Make me just like You.

*May the God of
peace Himself
sanctify you
completely.*
1 Thessalonians 5:23

A Prayer

O Lord, my heart and mind turn away so quickly
when I do not take time to be with You. Help me
slow down and sit at Your feet today.

My thoughts for Jesus

_____

_____

Tired of Being Good

February 9

Sometimes I get tired of being good. I feel worn out. But that's all right. God understands how I feel. He will help me to be good, even when I'm tired.

The everlasting God. . .neither faints nor is weary.
ISAIAH 40:28

A Prayer

O Jesus, You are everything I ever wanted. How I long to be with You. Please come and touch my heart with the livng water of Your new life today.

My thoughts for Jesus

_____

_____

There You Are

February 10

Lord, sometimes I can't imagine what You are like. But I want to be with You. Gentle breeze. Shining stars. Falling leaves. There You are, Lord. Everywhere I look, something reminds me of You.

Lift up your eyes on high, and see who has created these things.
ISAIAH 40:26

A Prayer

O Lord Jesus, I need You so much. Please pour the beauty of Your new life into my heart and mind so everything I say and do will be a blessing to You.

My thoughts for Jesus

_____

_____

Peace Like a River

February 11

God is bigger than me. He hung the stars in the sky. The sun shines with the light of His love. Every silver snowflake was made by the gentle touch of His hand. He will never leave me. I will trust in Him.

"You will keep him in perfect peace, whose mind is stayed on You."
ISAIAH 26:3

A Prayer

O Lord, please come and turn the bitter frozen winter in my heart into beautiful springtime. I want to be warm and clean and fresh and new.

My thoughts for Jesus

_____

_____

Do I Listen?

February 12

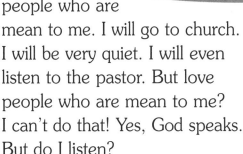

God speaks.
But do I listen?
He told me
to love even
people who are
mean to me. I will go to church.
I will be very quiet. I will even
listen to the pastor. But love
people who are mean to me?
I can't do that! Yes, God speaks.
But do I listen?

"You speak with us, and we will hear."
EXODUS 20:19

A Prayer

Jesus, I want to know You. But how can I know You if You won't show Yourself to me? O Lord, please come! I want to search and search until all I see is You.

My thoughts for Jesus

_____

_____

Busy, Busy!
February 13

I am so very
busy sometimes!
I must do this!
I must do that!
What's that, Lord?
What did You say? Speak
up! I can't hear You! Oops!
I have to go now. Give me
a call sometime. I'd really
love to talk to You. Bye!

*"Speak, for
Your servant
hears."*
1 SAMUEL 3:10

A Prayer

O Lord, thank You for the awesome power of Your
gentle voice. The thunder of your kindness shakes
the very earth. I will be quiet and listen for You.

My thoughts for Jesus

_____

_____

Stop, Look, Listen

February 14

Lord, where are You? I can't see You. I can't hear You. I don't know what to do. Please don't leave me here, God. I will be still. I will listen. I will wait. You will come.

"Whatever I tell you in the dark, speak in the light."
MATTHEW 10:27

A Prayer

Jesus, You are the Light of the World. When your holy light comes, darkness must run away. Please shine down on the dark places in my heart today.

My thoughts for Jesus

_____

_____

My Brother's Keeper

February 15

I am not perfect. Sometimes I get angry. Sometimes I make mistakes. Sometimes I even hurt my friends. I don't want to hurt my friends. I will do something special for them. I will show them God loves them.

None of us lives to himself.
ROMANS 14:7

A Prayer

O Lord, I know I don't deserve it. But thank You for taking such good care of me. Please teach me to be as patient with others as You are with me.

My thoughts for Jesus

_____

_____

I Must Get Up!

February 16

I give up!
I am frustrated.
My dreams will
never come
true. But God
says, "Try again."
He says, "Get up." He will
help me. He will make them
real. But first I must get up.

*"Arise from
the dead."*
EPHESIANS 5:14

A Prayer

O Lord, the bad things I want to see and say and
do get the best of me so often. Help me to stand
up and say no when I am tempted to do wrong.

My thoughts for Jesus

_____

_____

Get Going
February 17

I will get up.
I will get going.
There is no
reason to be
sad. Jesus is

with me. He will work
it out. Everything will be
okay. I think I'll make my
bed and go get a cookie.

"Arise and eat."
1 KINGS 19:5

A Prayer

O Lord, why is it so hard to love and forgive the
people who hurt me? Please help my "outside"
reflect the beauty You placed inside my heart.

My thoughts for Jesus

_____

_____

Don't Look Back
February 18

Oh no! What have I done? It's just no use. I've ruined everything! But Jesus will forgive me. He will take my awful mistakes and send them far away! I will give Jesus my broken heart. I will not look back. I will get up. I will take His hand. I will begin again.

"Rise, let us be going."
MATTHEW 26:46

A Prayer

O Jesus, I am so confused. I know I did the right thing. Why do I feel this way? Please take these swirling, stormy clouds and blow them far away.

My thoughts for Jesus

_____

_____

Shine

February 19

What do
I have to
do today?
Is it the very
same thing I did yesterday? Will
I do it all over again tomorrow?
Whatever it may be—here are my
hands, Lord. You take them. Help
me make something beautiful.

Arise, shine.
ISAIAH 60:1

Dreaming
February 20

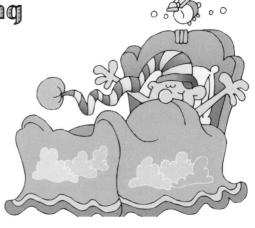

God gave me a wonderful dream! Oh, the places I'll go! Oh, the people I'll meet! I'd like to dream like this forever. But now it's time to wake up. It's time to do it!

"Arise, let us go from here."
JOHN 14:31

A Prayer

Jesus, please help me stop daydreaming about the good things You want me to do. Shake my sleepy head back to life so I can get up and do Your will.

My thoughts for Jesus

_____

_____

Now I've Done It!
February 21

Oh dear. Now I've done it. Just look at me! And look at this mess! I know I should try to be more careful. But I just got so excited. I love You so much. I had to show You! I know You understand. Even when I get too excited, You can use me.

"She has done a good work for Me."
MARK 14:6

A Prayer

Jesus, take my filthy, worn-out rags and wrap me in the beautiful new clothes of Your kindness and love. That is what people really long to see.

My thoughts for Jesus

_____

_____

Let Go!
February 22

I'm strong.
I'm tough.
I'm hanging
in there. I've
tied a knot

at the end of my rope, and I'm
hanging on! But did God tell me
to hang on? Or am I just afraid
to let go?

*Be still, and
know that I
am God.*
PSALM 46:10

A Prayer

O Lord, I am worried and upset, and my insides are
running around in crazy circles. Please touch me
with the courage to trust You completely today.

My thoughts for Jesus

_____

_____

When People Hurt Me

February 23

When I'm selfish
I break God's heart.
But Jesus forgives me.
He spread out His arms
and died for me. People may
hurt me. They may even make
me cry. But that's okay. I hurt
Jesus. But He died to take my
sins away. He forgave me. I will
forgive the people who hurt me.

*"The Son
of Man did not
come to
be served,
but to serve."*
MATTHEW 20:28

A Prayer

Jesus, Your love and kindness are all I need. I will
not try to find them in the heart or hands of any
person. That kind of love comes only from You.

My thoughts for Jesus

_____

_____

Help Yourself!

February 24

Here is my life,
Jesus. I will go
where You want
me to go. I will
do what You want
me to do. You can have
whatever You want, Lord.
Just help Yourself—to me!

*I will very gladly
spend and be spent
for your souls.*
2 CORINTHIANS 12:15

A Prayer

Jesus, thank You for taking such good care of me.
Let me spend each moment of this new day doing
and saying and being everything You want me to be.

My thoughts for Jesus

_____

_____

They Love Me Not

February 25

I want to tell them about Jesus. But what if they get mad at me? What if they laugh? What if they won't love me anymore? Oh, who cares if they love me or not? I love them. And I want them to know Jesus.

Though the more abundantly I love you, the less I am loved.
2 CORINTHIANS 12:15

A Prayer

Jesus, please take away forever the part of me that only cares about what I can get for myself. Give me a heart that is searching for You.

My thoughts for Jesus

_____

_____

You Can't Be Serious!

February 26

You want me to do what, God? I can't do that! It will never work! And how will I ever get it done? O God, when will I ever learn to trust You? And how long will it be before I realize that You can do what I cannot?

"Sir, You have nothing to draw with." JOHN 4:11

A Prayer

O Lord, what a joy it is to discover that You really are all I need. Thank You for the peace that comes from casting all my cares on You.

My thoughts for Jesus

_____

_____

Troubled Water

February 27

Why do I feel this way? Why does it hurt so much? Why won't anyone help? Maybe I should try to be strong. Maybe I should just try to do this by myself. No! I feel too empty inside. Only Jesus can help. He is God Almighty. And I will look to Him.

"Where then do You get that living water?" JOHN 4:11

A Prayer

O Lord, what joy it would bring to hear Your voice today. Please speak to me from Your Word as You teach me how to slow down and listen to You.

My thoughts for Jesus

_____

_____

What's the Big Idea?

February 28

I will do great
things for God!
I will dream up
a big idea. I will
ask God to bless it! It will be
big. It will be new! And it will
be wrong! Please forgive me,
Jesus. I put my big idea in
Your place inside my heart.
Something will always go wrong
with my big ideas. But I believe in You.

*Jesus answered
them, "Do you
now believe?"*
JOHN 16:31

A Prayer

Thank You, Jesus, for this beautiful new day and
all the good things in it. Raise me up and fill me
to overflowing with the power of Your new life.

My thoughts for Jesus

_____

_____

Mission Impossible

February 29

I can't ask
God to do that.
That would be
impossible!
You're right.
No one could do that.
No one but God. Go ahead.
Ask Him to do it! God will do
the impossible.

*"Lord, that
I may receive
my sight."*
LUKE 18:41

A Prayer

Jesus, I am Your beloved child. Beautiful like a lily.
Free like a sparrow. Strong like a tall tree planted by
the water. I thank You for the gift of new life.

My thoughts for Jesus

_____

_____

Do I Love Him?
March 1

I can do good.
I can be good.
Everyone may
think well of
me. And I can
say that I love
Him. But do I *really* love Him?

"Do you love Me?"
JOHN 21:17

A Prayer

O Lord, please lift the morning mist that keeps me from seeing You clearly. Shine Your strength and joy and new life into my heart today.

My thoughts for Jesus

_____

_____

Yes, I Love Him

March 2

It hurt when Jesus said, "Do you love Me?" Why would He say that? He knows I love Him. He knows I do! But that is why He asked. He knows. And now I know, too!

He said to him the third time, "Do you love Me?"
JOHN 21:17

A Prayer

Thank You, Jesus, for the courage You gave when I was afraid. Teach me to rain down Your treasure like a fountain on the lives of everyone around me.

My thoughts for Jesus

_____

_____

Feed My Sheep

March 3

Yes, Lord.
I do love
You! Now
I will feed
Your sheep.
You have
some funny sheep. But I will
love them all. I will love every
lumpy, dirty, lost, last one
of them.

*"Feed My
sheep."*
JOHN 21:17

A Prayer

Lord, let my thoughts and my words and the things
I choose to do fill the air around me with the beautiful, sweet perfume of Your perfect love.

My thoughts for Jesus

_____

_____

Father Knows Best

March 4

Where can God use me? What does He want me to do? I am good at many things. Things that would be very useful. But God does not care if I'm useful. He wants me to love Him. He wants me to be His.

"Nor do I count my life dear to myself."
ACTS 20:24

A Prayer

O Lord, open up my eyes so I can see how big You really are. Take my hand and lead me to the place where my heart is still and I can hear Your voice.

My thoughts for Jesus

_____

_____

Well Done!

March 5

God has a job for me. So I will do it! I may not be the very best. I may not always get it right. It may not go the way I planned. But God isn't worried about that. He just wants me to do it. He wants me to show Him I love Him.

". . .so that I may finish my race with joy." Acts 20:24

Same Old Thing
March 6

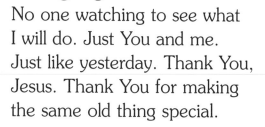

Nothing new today. No big plans. Nothing much going on. No one watching to see what I will do. Just You and me. Just like yesterday. Thank You, Jesus. Thank You for making the same old thing special.

. . .in much patience. . .
2 CORINTHIANS 6:4

A Prayer

O Lord, help me stop whining and complaining about everything and everyone around me. Teach my lips to bloom with a garden of thanks for all You have done.

My thoughts for Jesus

_____

_____

Surf's Up

March 7

Trouble will come. But I will not be afraid. The wind will blow. The waves will crash. I will not run away. I will grab my surfboard. I will run for the water. I will stand up and ride. Whee! Nothing can separate me from the love of God.

We are more than conquerors through Him who loved us.
ROMANS 8:37

A Prayer

Thank You, Jesus, for this life and the joy You bring. Thank You for my family and friends and for coming into my heart and making everything new.

My thoughts for Jesus

_____

_____

What God Wants

March 8

What does
God want?
Does He
want my
kindness?

My honesty? My good deeds?
No. He wants my sin. God
wants to take my sin away
and put Jesus in its place.

*"I have been
crucified with
Christ."*
GALATIANS 2:20

A Prayer

Thank You, Lord, for plowing up the hard places in
my heart. Thank You for the good seed You have
planted and the harvest of new life that will come.

My thoughts for Jesus

_____

_____

He Went That Way

March 9

I will walk with
Jesus. I will go
when He says,
"Go." I will stop
when He says,
"Stop." I don't

need to figure it all out. Jesus
loves me. I can trust Him. He
will lead me home.

*"Do you
also want
to go away?"*
JOHN 6:67

A Prayer

Jesus, please forgive me. I have been spending so
little time with You. Thank You for the cross. Thank
You for saving me. Fill me with Your Spirit again.

My thoughts for Jesus

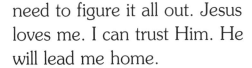

_____

_____

Be a Message

March 10

God gave me a message. He gave me His Word. And the  Word of God can change lives. But first it must change me. Yes, God gave me a message. And if I let Him, He will make me a message, too. My life will tell everyone that God loves them.

Preach the word!
2 TIMOTHY 4:2

A Prayer

O Lord, help me to worship, work, and play in a way that is pleasing to You today. Open my eyes to the beauty of Your new life springing up all around me.

My thoughts for Jesus

_____

_____

What God Sees
March 11

I know God
has a plan for
me. And He
will make it happen. It may take
a long time. But I can wait. I will
let Jesus plant me, just like a seed.
Sometimes a seed takes a long
time to grow. But God knows the
right time. One day I will blossom
and bring forth fruit.

"I was not disobedient to the heavenly vision. . ."
ACTS 26:19

A Prayer

O Lord, please come and breathe the breath of
new life over me until my heart and my mind and
my body are healed and whole and alive once more.

My thoughts for Jesus

_____

_____

What's in It for Me?

I love to give. I would give Jesus anything. Even myself. For He always gives so much in return. But I will not treat Jesus like a bubble-gum machine. I love Him for who He is. Not for what I get out of Him.

> "See, we have left all and followed You."
> MARK 10:28

A Prayer

Jesus, please touch Your flame to the lamp of my heart. Burn up the darkness around me with the blazing light of Your Holy Spirit.

My thoughts for Jesus

_____

_____

Clean!
March 13

I can be good.
I can obey.
I can mind my
manners. But
I need to do something even
more important. I can forget
about me and get caught up
in the wonder of Jesus! I can
give myself to Him. Just like
He gave me Himself.

*"God so
loved the
world that
He gave. . ."*
JOHN 3:16

A Prayer

O Lord, please forgive me. I've done so many bad
things. Thank You for rolling up the past and
throwing it out for good. I want to be like You.

My thoughts for Jesus

_____

_____

Who Has My Heart?

March 14

Who has my
heart? What
have I given
it to? Have
I given it to
anger? To being important?
To having lots of things?
Jesus made my heart. But
have I given it back to Him?

*You are that
one's slaves
whom you obey.*
ROMANS 6:16

A Prayer

O Lord, I want so many things that I don't really
need. Please teach me to give freely and not keep
Your blessings hidden away just for myself.

My thoughts for Jesus

_____

_____

Where Are We Going?

March 15

Where are we
going? What
is Jesus doing?
Why doesn't He
stop? Why won't He wait? Why
has He gone so far ahead?
I thought I knew Him. I thought
He loved me. How can I follow
Him now? O Lord, forgive me.
It is so dark. And I am so afraid.
I will be still. I will trust You. You are God.

*And as they
followed they
were afraid.*
MARK 10:32

A Prayer

Jesus, this day is in Your hands. Tomorrow will be, too.
So I will relax and trust You. You are God Almighty.
And You have already taken care of tomorrow.

My thoughts for Jesus

_____

_____

Into the Light

March 16

What am
I hiding?
What lives
deep down
in the secret
darkness of
my heart? Is it anger?
Unforgiveness? Do I want to
hurt my friend? I will drag those
things out into God's light. I will
let Him change my heart.

For we must all appear before the judgment seat of Christ.
2 CORINTHIANS 5:10

A Prayer

Thank You, Lord, for the peace Your love has placed
in my heart. Please help my "outsides" catch up to
my "insides" so I can share that peace with others.

My thoughts for Jesus

First Things First
March 17

I want to do
good. I want
to help.
I want to
share God's
love. I want to
tell others about Jesus.
But I will not give my heart
to any of these things. My
heart belongs to Jesus.

*Therefore we
make it our
aim. . .to be well
pleasing to Him.*
2 CORINTHIANS 5:9

A Prayer

O Jesus, I want to see Your face. Please fill my
heart with the joy that comes from knowing You
are God Almighty and You are here right now.

My thoughts for Jesus

_____

_____

Have It Your Way
March 18

How do I look?
What do you
see? Do you
see Jesus—or
do you see me?
do you see me?
I will let Jesus wash me.
Jesus knows where I need
to be washed inside. I know,
too. And I want to be clean.

*. . .perfecting
holiness in the
fear of God.*
2 Corinthians 7:1

A Prayer

O Jesus, please forgive me. I have been foolish and angry, and I am so ashamed. Please help me to reflect more of Your beauty and less of my beast.

My thoughts for Jesus

_____

_____

Lead Me On

March 19

Where are
we going?
I don't really
know! But
God knows.
And I know Him. So I will
keep on walking. God is real.
God is here. Jesus loves me.
Everything will be all right.

*He went out,
not knowing
where he was
going.*
HEBREWS 11:8

A Prayer

Thank You, Lord Jesus, for walking with me today and for making every place we go come alive with the blessing and radiant beauty of Your new life.

My thoughts for Jesus

_____

_____

Decisions, Decisions!

March 20

What does God want? What is God's will? God's will is me! And He has set me free. I am not afraid to decide. Jesus loves me. If I am wrong, He will show me. And I will stop.

"Shall I hide from Abraham what I am doing?"
GENESIS 18:17

A Prayer

Thank You, Lord, for watching over this house day and night. Thank You for protecting me and making me into everything your heart desires.

My thoughts for Jesus

_____

_____

I'm with Him

March 21

Jesus died
on the cross
to take away
my sins. He
did it for me.
And now He wants
to live in me, too. Please
come into my heart, Lord
Jesus. Oh, how I love You.

*"I have been
crucified with
Christ."*
GALATIANS 2:20

A Prayer

Thank You, Jesus, for changing my life. Thank You
for making my heart Your home. Thank you for the
love I do not deserve. Please make me more like You.

My thoughts for Jesus

_____

_____

A Burning Heart

March 22

God's love is like a fire burning in my heart. It lights up every dreary place. It melts the coldest frozen heart. Its gentle warmth and beautiful fragrance are the light and life of every plain old, bald, and boring day.

"Did not our heart burn within us?" LUKE 24:32

A Prayer

This is the day the Lord has made. Let the memory of Your love and all the good things You do for me today sparkle like a jewel in my heart forever.

My thoughts for Jesus

_____

_____

I Was Wrong
March 23

I was wrong.
I know what
I did. I know
it was a mistake.
I did it anyway.
But I won't make
excuses. There's nothing
to explain. Please forgive
me. I was wrong.

*Where there are
envy, strife, and
divisions among
you, are you
not carnal?*
1 CORINTHIANS 3:3

A Prayer

O Lord, Your love is amazing. Thank You for patiently showing me the way You want me to go even while I am trying so hard to run the other way.

My thoughts for Jesus

_____

_____

Let It Happen
March 24

I told her about Jesus. And she got mad! I know God is changing her heart. And that hurts. I'd like to make it better. But I won't. I will get out of God's way. I will let God plow her up so He can plant new seed in her. Soon Jesus will grow tall and strong in her broken heart.

"He must increase, but I must decrease."
JOHN 3:30

A Prayer

O Lord, thank You for the fire of Your Holy Spirit that burns away my desire to point out other people's faults and cover up my own.

My thoughts for Jesus

_____

_____

Don't Look at Me
March 25

I want to be good. I want to be kind. But not so you will look at me. Not even to show you what God can do. Was I standing in front of Jesus? I'm sorry. I will sit down. Now maybe you can see Him.

The friend of the bridegroom. . .
JOHN 3:29

A Prayer

Jesus, please forgive me. I am busy and distracted and have forgotten to take time to be with You. Teach me how to live simply. Hide me deep inside Your heart.

My thoughts for Jesus

_____

_____

Pure in Heart

March 26

I can't do that anymore. It's not really bad. It's not really wrong. But it just doesn't feel right. I guess it's okay for other people. But when I do it, I feel like I've broken God's heart. I'm just not going to do that anymore.

"Blessed are the pure in heart, for they shall see God."
MATTHEW 5:8

A Prayer

O Lord, I am frightened by how easily I forget You. Help me live this day in the pure light of a heart that is powerfully and completely in love with You.

My thoughts for Jesus

_____

_____

Good Enough Yet?

March 27

Am I good
enough yet?
Am I doing all
right? I could
be more polite.
I could read more
and pray more and give more
and do more. But most of all,
I could look to Jesus more. Then
I could get to know Him better.

*"Come up
here, and
I will show you
things."*
REVELATION 4:1

A Prayer

O Lord, please take away the fog and flurries that blur my vision of You today. Thank You for a clean heart and a clear mind that is focused only on You.

My thoughts for Jesus

_____

_____

Faith
March 28

I know what God wants. But how will I do it? I can study and plan. I can think through the good and bad. But that is not faith. I don't understand. But God does. I can trust Him. He loves me. I will do what He says. I feel happy inside when I follow Him.

The disciples said to Him, ". . .are You going there again?"
JOHN 11:8

A Prayer

O Jesus, I need You more than anything. I don't need to be important. I don't care if anyone ever knows my name. I just want to get closer to You.

My thoughts for Jesus

_____

_____

Knock, Knock

March 29

Surprise! Where
will I find Jesus
today? Who knows?
He could be anywhere!
In anything or anyone. His
love is bigger than my church.
Bigger than my ideas. Bigger
than any endless winter sky.
He is alive inside of my heart.
I will look for Him everywhere.

*"Therefore
you also
be ready."*
LUKE 12:40

A Prayer

Jesus, I am ready and waiting for You to come.
So come with power. Come, mighty King. I am
ready to do what You want me to do.

My thoughts for Jesus

_____

_____

I Will Pray

March 30

I will pray for her. I will not get angry. I will not talk behind her back. I think something must be wrong. Something is breaking her heart. I will ask God to help her. I know God has a plan for her life. And He wants me to help— He wants me to pray for her.

He. . . wondered that there was no intercessor. ISAIAH 59:16

A Prayer

Thank You, Lord, for the gentle hands that paint the night with stars. Sing Your love song deep into my waiting heart and breathe new life in me.

My thoughts for Jesus

_____

_____

Me First
March 31

God will fix him! He's creepy and mean and he never says anything nice, and he just makes me so mad! Yes, God will fix him! But maybe God should fix me first. Then I can pray for this person.

If anyone sees his brother sinning. . .
1 JOHN 5:16

A Prayer

Thank You, Jesus, for light and joy and health and blessing. Rise up in my heart and shine the warm light of Your beauty in and out of everything I do.

My thoughts for Jesus

_____

_____

Have a Heart
April 1

God's Word
can change
the hardest
heart. But
I will not use
it like a spear to stab my
enemy. I will speak God's
truth with love. And then
I will remember to pray.

*Christ makes
intercession
for us.*
ROMANS 8:34

A Prayer

Search me, Lord Jesus. Make Your way down to the
deepest, darkest place in my heart and pray until
a clear spring is flowing from my life into Yours.

My thoughts for Jesus

_____

_____

Now I See
April 2

Once
I couldn't see
Jesus. I wanted
to have lots of
things. I wanted
people to like me.
I wanted everyone to do
what I said. But something
happened. I put all that
down. And now I can see.
Now I can see Jesus.

*"The Lord Jesus
. . .has sent me
that you may
receive your
sight."*
Acts 9:17

A Prayer

O Lord, I once was blind. But now I see Your strength
when I am weak, Your joy when I am afraid, and Your
hope when I am ready to give up. You are all I need.

My thoughts for Jesus

_____

_____

If Only
April 3

Why did I do that? What was I thinking? How can God love me when I make the same awful mistakes over and over again? I don't want to think about it! But I must. And then I must let Him change my heart.

"If you had known. . . the things that make for your peace!"
LUKE 19:42

A Prayer

O Lord, I need Your help. I don't know what to do. Please take away the mask that is covering up the truth. Show me what You want and I will do it.

My thoughts for Jesus

_____

_____

Trust or Bust

April 4

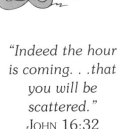

Where did God go? Why isn't He blessing my plans? How can I trust Him if He won't bless me? How can I trust Him if He won't make me happy? How can I say that I love Him when all I care about are His blessings?

"Indeed the hour is coming. . .that you will be scattered."
JOHN 16:32

A Prayer

O Lord, I need You so much. Please come into every cup and can and corner of this new day and fill it with Your beauty and power, mighty King.

My thoughts for Jesus

_____

_____

Gethsemane

April 5

Jesus was alone in the garden. But why was
He crying? It was my sin. He knew He was
about to die. He knew He would be nailed to
the cross. But He did nothing wrong! It was
all my fault. He would die because of my sins.
And His death would take my sins away! How
could He love me that much? I don't know.
But He did. Jesus is God's Son.

But He lived as a man. He died
as a man. And because He did,
I will see the face of God.

*Jesus came
with them to. . .
Gethsemane*
MATTHEW 26:36

A Prayer

O Jesus, I have been so slow to thank You for all
the good things You've done for me. Here I am, Lord.
Take me in Your arms. I love You with all my heart.

My thoughts for Jesus

_____

_____

The Cross

April 6

Jesus was
born to die
on the cross.
It was not
an accident.
It did not
happen to Him.
Jesus went there
on purpose. He
went there for me.

*. . .who Himself bore
our sins in His own
body on the tree.*
1 PETER 2:24

A Prayer

Jesus, You are bigger than any problem I will face
today. So I will thank You and I will rest. I know You
will take care of me. Everything will be all right.

My thoughts for Jesus

_____

_____

Show and Tell

April 7

The Bible can be hard to understand. And God's heart can be hard to find. But God is not hiding from me. He is calling me closer. When I dare to look for Him, the flower of His Word will begin to bloom inside of my heart.

He commanded them that they should tell no one the things they had seen.
MARK 9:9

A Prayer

O Lord, smooth out my rough edges. Soften up my prickly parts. Polish every dull and dirty surface until I reflect Your glorious light to everyone I meet.

My thoughts for Jesus

_____

_____

To Rise Again
April 8

Jesus died on the cross. But He rose again! God gave Him new life. Now Jesus wants to give His new life to me. He wants to nail my sin to the cross. He wants to leave it there to die. He wants to put His life in its place. He wants to make me His child.

"Ought not the Christ to have suffered these things. . . ?"
LUKE 24:26

A Prayer

O Jesus, here is my heart. Seep through every window and door and fill me with the joy that comes from knowing You are here right now.

My thoughts for Jesus

_____

_____

Have I Seen Him?
April 9

God is good.
I have every-
thing I need.
I see His
blessings each
and every day. But
have I ever looked
beyond His blessings?
Beyond what He gives?
Have I ever seen Him?
I want to see Jesus.

*He appeared in
another form to
two of them.*
MARK 16:12

A Prayer
O Lord, please come and speak Your peace into my
heart. Teach me to be quiet long enough to know
when You are near. I want to hear Your voice today.

My thoughts for Jesus

_____

_____

What to Do with Sin
April 10

Sin is anything that breaks God's heart. And I have sinned. But what should I do about it? Should I try to quit? Should I find something better to do? No! My sin must be killed! I must let God nail it to the cross.

Our old man was crucified with Him. . . that we should no longer be slaves of sin.
ROMANS 6:6

A Prayer

O Lord, thank You for the power to rise above the wind and rain that have blown so quickly into this day. You shine above and in spite of it, and I can, too.

My thoughts for Jesus

_____

_____

Come On In!

April 11

Here is my heart, Jesus. Please make my heart Your home. Fill every closet and cupboard. Invade every dark and empty room with the blazing light of Your love.

We also shall be in the likeness of His resurrection.
ROMANS 6:5

A Prayer

O Lord, thank You for wrapping Your mighty arms around me and for holding me so close that when people look for me, the only thing they find is You.

My thoughts for Jesus

_____

_____

The Gift
April 12

God does not *give* me eternal life. He *is* eternal life! What He gives me is Himself. He comes to live inside of me.

Death no longer has dominion over Him.
ROMANS 6:9

A Prayer

O Lord, how I love to feel the joy that comes when You give me the things I ask for. Help me enjoy Your gifts without letting them turn my heart from You.

My thoughts for Jesus

_____

_____

He Is Strong!

April 13

I know what
God wants me
to do. It won't
be easy. And
the load will be heavy.
But I can do it. I will not let it
crush me. I will put one end on
God's shoulders. He is strong.
Together we will get it done.

*Cast your
burden on
the LORD.*
PSALM 55:22

A Prayer

Jesus, please come and surprise me with Your
gentle Spirit today. Touch my hand. Call out my
name. Oh, the joy of simply knowing You are here.

My thoughts for Jesus

_____

_____

Squeezed
April 14

Sometimes it hurts. But I will not complain. Jesus loves me. And He is working to make something wonderful. But to get the juice, the grapes must be squeezed! I won't whine when I feel squeezed.

"Take My yoke upon you and learn from Me."
MATTHEW 11:29

A Prayer

Jesus, please forgive me. I have wandered far from You. Take this dried-up, lifeless desert-heart and make it bloom once more with the flower of new life.

My thoughts for Jesus

_____

_____

Does He?

April 15

What's the big deal? God doesn't care if I do that, does He? I'm sure it won't matter. Or will it? I don't really know. But I am His. And I'm not going to do it until I'm sure.

The heart of Asa was loyal all his days. 2 CHRONICLES 15:17

A Prayer

O Lord, please shine Your light through me today. Let the things I say and do make Your heart smile. I love you with all my heart.

My thoughts for Jesus

_____

_____

Come On Down!

April 16

I feel great today! And I'd like to feel this way forever. But I can't. Sooner or later I will have to get up off my cloud and come down from the mountain. God is on the mountain. But He is in the valley, as well.

"While you have the light, believe in the light." JOHN 12:36

A Prayer

O Lord, let the words I speak, the things I think, and the way I feel inside fill the air around me with the beautiful, sweet smell of Your amazing love.

My thoughts for Jesus

_____

_____

Be God's
April 17

I am God's.
I will get out
of the boat.
I will run to
Him across
the water. The
water is deep. But He can
do anything. He won't let
me sink. He is calling. And
I must go!

*He put on his
outer garment. . .
and plunged
into the sea.*
JOHN 21:7

A Prayer

O Lord, forgive me. I let the stinky smell of worry,
fear, and doubt sneak out. Please come and clear
the air with a fresh breath of courage and trust.

My thoughts for Jesus

_____

_____

Ready or Not
April 18

I am ready, Lord. Ready to do something great and big and amazing. Ready to do something so small that no one will ever notice. Here I am. You can send me.

God called to him. . . . And he said, "Here I am."
EXODUS 3:4

A Prayer

Jesus, I want to be completely Yours. Teach me to soak up Your Word like a sponge soaks up water so You can squeeze out new life to everyone I meet.

My thoughts for Jesus

_____

_____

Not to Me
April 19

Many things will try to pull me away from God. Have I done something hard for Him? Good! But now I must watch out for the little things—the things that don't seem to matter. Sometimes they can be the most dangerous trap of all!

For Joab had defected to Adonijah, though he had not defected to Absalom.
1 KINGS 2:28

A Prayer

O Lord, let the words I speak today shine with the brilliant light of Your mighty power. Draw me deep inside Your heart so others may find You there.

My thoughts for Jesus

_____

_____

Worry!

April 20

Why am
I worried?
Why am
I afraid?
Why do
I think that

God will forget about me?
O Lord, please forgive me!
You have not forgotten me.
But I have forgotten You.

*For all the
promises of God
in Him are Yes,
and in Him Amen.*
2 CORINTHIANS 1:20

A Prayer

Thank You, Jesus, for the peace and joy that fill
this new day because You are alive and You are
here and You are everything I will ever need.

My thoughts for Jesus

_____

_____

Don't Hurt Him Now!

April 21

"What about this? What about that? First show me, and then I'll believe!" Am I hurting Jesus with the questions I ask? He loves me. He will take care of me. He is here.

"Have I been with you so long, and yet you have not known Me, Philip?"
JOHN 14:9

A Prayer

O Lord, thank You for the mighty arms that draw me closer and closer to You. How I long to see You face-to-face. Please make me more like You.

My thoughts for Jesus

_____

_____

Good-bye
April 22

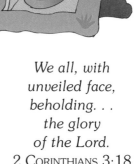

I miss my friend. She meant so much to me. She showed me how to be like Jesus. And now she is gone. But God meant for her to go. God doesn't want me to trust in my friend. He wants me to trust in Him.

We all, with unveiled face, beholding. . . the glory of the Lord.
2 CORINTHIANS 3:18

A Prayer

O Lord, thank You for the cross. Thank You for the blood that washed my sins away. I love You more than anything. And now I know You love me, too.

My thoughts for Jesus

_____

_____

Worship and Work

April 23

Here are my hands, Lord. Use them to make some-thing beautiful. And here is my heart, too. Help me to fall in love with You. Help me not to love the good things I do more than I love You.

For we are God's fellow workers.
1 CORINTHIANS 3:9

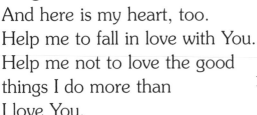

A Prayer

Jesus, I need You in so many ways. Oh, how I thank You for never hiding Your face or turning me away when I come running to You.

My thoughts for Jesus

_____

_____

What to Want
April 24

I can work hard.
I can do a good
job. People will
like what I do.
But God does not want me
to care what people think.
He wants me to love them.
He wants me to show some-
one else the way home to Him.

"Nevertheless do not rejoice in this, that the spirits are subject to you." LUKE 10:20

A Prayer

O Jesus, my friend is hurting. I want to help. But I don't know what to do. Please soften her heart so she will let You come in and sweep the pain away.

My thoughts for Jesus

_____

_____

In the Mood
April 25

I'm just not
in the mood
right now.
I know what
I need to do.
And I don't really want to
do it. But I will do it. God
gave me His best. So I will
give Him my best. Even
when I feel like I do today.

*Be ready
in season and
out of season.*
2 TIMOTHY 4:2

A Prayer

O Lord, I am tied up and tangled in the web of my
own foolish choices. Please help me fix the terrible
mess I have made. I want to be beautiful again.

My thoughts for Jesus

_____

_____

Abraham Trusted God

April 26

Abraham loved God. He was ready to do anything God asked. Even if it meant going against everything he had come to believe. Beliefs can be wrong. Abraham did not trust his beliefs. Abraham trusted God.

"Take now your son. . . ."
GENESIS 22:2

A Prayer

Lord Jesus, here is my heart. Please take away my desire to be right all the time and lead me to the place where I can rest and hear Your voice.

My thoughts for Jesus

_____

_____

What Do I Want?

April 27

I want to do great things. And God may let me. But great things come and great things go. Sometimes they're just an accident. God never gives me anything by accident. God gave me Jesus. But do I want Him?

"Do you seek great things for yourself?"
JEREMIAH 45:5

A Prayer

O Lord, help me clothe myself with kindness today so that the words I speak bring Your light and love to everyone who hears them.

My thoughts for Jesus

_____

_____

What I Will Get

April 28

God is greater than the greatest thing I will ever do. He is more valuable than any good thing that will ever be put into my hands. I will stop worrying so much about things. I will give Jesus my heart.

"I will give your life to you as a prize in all places, wherever you go."
JEREMIAH 45:5

A Prayer

O Jesus, I love You so much. How I long for You to touch my heart and clear away the angry black clouds that keep me from simply being Your child.

My thoughts for Jesus

_____

_____

Un-Certainly!
April 29

Who knows
what will
happen
today? God
knows! God
knows what to do.
God knows which way
to go. *God knows.* And
He loves me. I will trust
Him and take the next step.

*It has not yet
been revealed
what we shall be.*
1 JOHN 3:2

A Prayer

O Lord, You are amazing. How can I ever thank
You enough for touching me, changing my heart,
taking my sins away, and making everything new?

My thoughts for Jesus

_____

_____

Real Love
April 30

I can love. I don't have to hate. I don't have to get angry. God's love is flowing through me like a wild river. I forget to love. I get filled up with selfishness. But when I open my heart, God's river of love comes pouring into me. At last I can love.

Love suffers long and is kind.
1 CORINTHIANS 13:4

A Prayer

O Jesus, please come and fill me with Your Spirit today. Give me new strength and a quiet heart that is light and free and eager to trust in You.

My thoughts for Jesus

_____

_____

Lights, Camera. . .

May 1

In my heart
I want to do
good. And
with that very
same heart I long
for people to notice me.
That is not right. I am not
an angel. I am just a child.
A child God can use. Even
if no one is looking.

*For we walk
by faith,
not by sight.*
2 CORINTHIANS 5:7

A Prayer

O Lord, how I thank You for the radiant joy You
have poured into my heart today. Visit my inner
kingdom and fill it with Your peace.

My thoughts for Jesus

_____

_____

Patience

May 2

I can wait.
God is faithful.
He will do what
He says He
will do!

"Though it tarries, wait for it."
HABAKKUK 2:3

A Prayer

Jesus, I love You with all my heart. Please teach me how to put up with other people and treat them with kindness no matter how they treat me.

My thoughts for Jesus

_____

_____

Pray for Her!

May 3

I will pray for her. I will pray that God will change her heart. And if God has to break her heart to change it, I will let Him. I won't get in the way. I won't try to help. If I let Him, God will do something beautiful.

Praying always with all prayer and supplication in the Spirit.
EPHESIANS 6:18

A Prayer

O Lord, teach me to be sensitive to the needs of the people around me. Please give me the courage and the desire to bring those needs to You in prayer.

My thoughts for Jesus

_____

_____

Pray for Him!
May 4

Sometimes I want my own way. I want God to do what I want. I want Him to make people act the way I want them to. I need to stop being so stubborn. I need to be more like Jesus.

Having boldness to enter the Holiest by the blood of Jesus.
HEBREWS 10:19

A Prayer

O Lord, You have promised me so many good things. But Your answer seems so far away. Teach me to wait patiently for You to come.

My thoughts for Jesus

_____

_____

Tell Him!
May 5

I will tell him about Jesus. I don't need to change his mind. I don't need to point out every little sin. The love of God's Holy Spirit will do all that. But first I must tell him that Jesus loves him.

For the time has come for judgment to begin at the house of God.
1 PETER 4:17

A Prayer

O Jesus, I need You so much. Please come with Your saving power. Move in and out and all around until my heart is as light and lifted up as Yours.

My thoughts for Jesus

_____

_____

Tell Her!
May 6

I will tell her about Jesus. She may not like it. She may not want to hear. But God was patient with me. So I will be patient with her. I will tell her. God will bring her home.

Stand fast therefore in the liberty by which Christ has made us free.
GALATIANS 5:1

A Prayer

O Lord, what a joy it is to know that I am Your beloved child. Teach me to turn away from anything that would try to tear us apart.

My thoughts for Jesus

_____

_____

This Old House

May 7

What am
I building?
And whose
idea was it?
One day God will inspect my
work. If it was done His way,
it will be allowed to stand. But
if it was not—if I never asked
God what He wanted—it will
have to be knocked down.

*"Sit down
first and
count
the cost."*
LUKE 14:28

A Prayer

O Lord, here is my heart. Lead me and guide me.
Teach me to do Your will. Fill me with Your mighty
power. I want to be like You.

My thoughts for Jesus

_____

_____

Ready, Aim. . .

May 8

I am like a bow and arrow in God's hands. God stretches and pulls. At times I feel like I will break. But God does not stop. He keeps on stretching. God can see the target. He will hit it. When He is ready I will fly!

"Because you have kept My command to persevere. . ."
REVELATION 3:10

A Prayer

O Jesus, You are so good to me. Please help me to give as freely, to love as patiently, and to deal as kindly with others as You do with me.

My thoughts for Jesus

_____

_____

Don't Lose Your Vision

May 9

God is alive
in everything
I do. He's in
the great big
important things.
He's in the little things, too.
I can trust Him when my work
is easy. And I can trust Him
when the goal looks like it's
still a million miles away.

*Where there is
no revelation,
the people
cast off
restraint.*
PROVERBS 29:18

A Prayer

O Lord, teach me to follow Your footsteps like a beloved child and not to stumble blindly along like a wild animal with no direction and no master.

My thoughts for Jesus

_____

_____

Just Do It!

May 10

I know what
God wants.
So I'm going
to get up and
do it. I won't
put it off. I won't
be afraid. I won't wonder,
or worry, or look for God
to give me a special message.
I will trust Him. I will do it!

*Add to
your faith
virtue.*
2 PETER 1:5

A Prayer

Thank You, Lord Jesus, for the beautiful new life
that healed this fragile little temple and made its
light shine like the sun with Your kindness and love.

My thoughts for Jesus

_____

_____

Him!
May 11

God, I can't love him. He's selfish and mean. Just like I was. Just like I am. But You love me anyway. Your love changed my heart. It can change his, too. So I will love him. Just like You loved me.

Add to your. . .brotherly kindness love.
2 PETER 1:5, 7

A Prayer

O Lord, You are beautiful. Thank You for touching my life with Your mighty power and love. How I long to see You face-to-face. You are all I will ever need.

My thoughts for Jesus

_____

_____

Having No Habits
May 12

God does not
want to give me
good habits. God
wants to change
my heart. My good
habits shout, "Look at me!"
I may pay more attention to
my good habits than I do to
God. God wants me to look
only at Him. He wants to put
Jesus in place of my habits.

*For if these
things are yours
and abound, you
will be neither
barren nor
unfruitful.*
2 PETER 1:8

A Prayer

Thank You, Lord, for a brave new heart and a mind
that is open to hear Your truth. Soften and shape
my life with Your Word so I can be like You.

My thoughts for Jesus

_____

_____

Easy Does It

May 13

God's gentle voice is whispering in my ear. He is showing me the right thing to do. I will listen when God speaks. His commands are easy to keep. All I have to do is say, "Okay!"

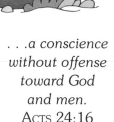

. . .a conscience without offense toward God and men.
ACTS 24:16

A Prayer

O Jesus, please come and bathe me in the waves of Your healing power until every inch of my body is healed and whole and singing Your praise.

My thoughts for Jesus

_____

_____

Even Here

May 14

I don't like
this very much.
In fact, I don't
like it at all.
But here I am.
God put me here for a reason.
I will let His tender love pour
out of my heart—even here.

*. . .that the
life of Jesus
also may be
manifested
in our body.*
2 CORINTHIANS 4:10

A Prayer

Thank You, Jesus, for pouring Your new life into my
heart and for breathing the beautiful breath of
freedom that saved me and washed my sins away.

My thoughts for Jesus

_____

_____

Powerhouse!

May 15

I will give away what God has given me! God put His love in my heart. Now I must give it away to someone else. I must let His love pour back out through my hands and my feet and my heart and my mouth.

. . .that you may know what is the hope of His calling.
EPHESIANS 1:18

A Prayer

O Lord, I am having such a hard time being all You want me to be. Please fill me with Your power so I can be a real joy to Your heart.

My thoughts for Jesus

_____

_____

Everything I Need

May 16

God loves me.
He knows what
I need. Every star
in the sky lights
the night with His
love. He made each tiny grain
of sand. God knows where I am.
God hears when I pray. He will
give me everything I need.

*. . .partakers
of the
divine
nature. . .*
2 PETER 1:4

A Prayer

Thank You, Jesus, for touching this day with the
sweetness of Your power. Let me be as big and
bold and fearless and free as You are today.

My thoughts for Jesus

_____

_____

Son of Man
May 17

How much does
Jesus love me?
He loves me so much
He became a man. He stepped
out of heaven. He stepped into
a human body! He gave up being
with God to become like me.
And because He did, one day
I will step out of my body and
step into heaven with Him.

He was parted from them and carried up into heaven.
LUKE 24:51

A Prayer

O Lord, I need You more than anything or anyone else in the whole world. Here is my heart. Fill me to overflowing with Your goodness and beauty.

My thoughts for Jesus

_____

_____

Consider the Lilies
May 18

Birds do not
worry. Stars
don't get upset.
Lilies don't
hurry from this
thing to that. But every
last one is alive with God's
love. I don't need to be useful.
I just need to be His!

*"Consider
the lilies of
the field."*
MATTHEW
6:28

A Prayer

Thank You, Jesus, for Your kindness and patience.
You are my Father. Forgive me for trying so hard
to do what You have already done.

My thoughts for Jesus

_____

_____

Together

May 19

Trouble will come. But I will not be afraid. God is here. He is bigger than any trouble. Nothing will ever separate me from His love. My hand is in His. We will go through this together. And we will reach the other side of the trouble.

Who shall separate us from the love of Christ?
ROMANS 8:35

A Prayer

O Lord, how I thank You for the good work You give. But deep inside I feel it may be time for something new. Please show me Your way and I will follow You.

My thoughts for Jesus

_____

_____

I Can Do All Things
May 20

I can do it—I know
I can! Jesus is alive
inside my heart.
I will never say,
"I can't." "I can't"
just means "I won't."
Sometimes I feel so grumpy
or sad or lazy. But no matter
how I feel, Jesus says I can do
all things—when I trust in Him!

"By your patience possess your souls." LUKE 21:19

A Prayer

Thank You, Jesus, for being so patient with me as I fumble and stumble my way into becoming the person You want me to be on the inside and out.

My thoughts for Jesus

_____

_____

Everything

May 21

Why should
I worry? Jesus
loves me. He
will give me
everything I need.
I won't waste my time
worrying about how to get
more things. I don't need
more things. I need Jesus.

*"But seek first the
kingdom of God. . . ."*
MATTHEW 6:33

A Prayer

O Lord, protect me from the sights and sounds
that long to tear me away from You. Untangle me
from this mess and fill me with Your Spirit again.

My thoughts for Jesus

_____

_____

Why?
May 22

Why do I feel so lonely? What is God doing? God is answering prayer! Jesus prayed that I would be one with the Father just like He is. And now God is answering His prayer. He is letting me feel lonely so I will go closer to Him.

". . .that they all may be one."
JOHN 17:21

A Prayer

O Lord, please forgive me for allowing my heart to turn sour and dry. I want to bud and blossom with Your beauty and sweetness again.

My thoughts for Jesus

_____

_____

Careful Now!

May 23

I can be
very careful.
I can worry
over every
little thing.
I can grumble

and groan over every
last wee, teeny, tiny,
small thing. Or I can
trust in Him.

*"Do not
worry about
your life."*
MATTHEW 6:25

A Prayer

O Jesus, what a joy it is to know that You are God Almighty and You are taking care of me. Breathe Your new life into my heart. I want to worship You.

My thoughts for Jesus

_____

_____

Fall Down, Go Boom

May 24

O God, I have made so many mistakes. I want to be good. I want to do the right thing. Why can't I do it? Why is it so hard? Over and over again I fail. But You reach out Your hand. You take me in Your arms. Your tender love melts my fear away. O God, You are so big. And I am so small. Please forgive me. I want to be like You.

And when I saw Him, I fell at His feet as dead.
REVELATION 1:17

A Prayer

Thank You, Jesus, for changing my heart. Take this little house and make it as clean and bright and beautiful as You are.

My thoughts for Jesus

_____

_____

Very Interesting
May 25

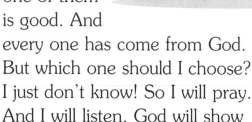

Look at all these beautiful things! Every one of them is good. And every one has come from God. But which one should I choose? I just don't know! So I will pray. And I will listen. God will show me what to do.

"If you take the left, then I will go to the right. . ."
GENESIS 13:9

A Prayer

O Jesus, I want to be more like You. Teach me to recognize Your voice. Help me know when You are near. Take our hearts and make them beat as one.

My thoughts for Jesus

_____

_____

Don't Stop Now!

May 26

Jesus said pray—and
never stop! So that's
just what I will do. I will
tell Him every good thing
that makes me happy. I will
tell Him every sad thing that
breaks my heart. He wants
to hear me. He wants to listen.
So I will tell Him! Twenty-four hours every
day—anytime, anywhere, anything, any way!
I will never, ever, ever stop. I will pray!

*Pray without
ceasing.*
1 THESSALONIANS
5:17

A Prayer

O Lord, so many people need the new life only You
can give. Help me not to lose hope but to look to
You and pray expecting a miracle.

My thoughts for Jesus

_____

_____

He Is Here
May 27

Jesus is here. His Holy Spirit is alive deep inside my heart. He will teach me right from wrong. He will hold me when I am afraid. He is never far away. Right now—right this very minute—Jesus is here!

"...endued with power from on high."
LUKE 24:49

A Prayer

O Lord, let me be the living, breathing example of Your Word that says, "Not by might, nor by power, but by My Spirit, says the Lord."

My thoughts for Jesus

_____

_____

No Doubt about It

May 28

Jesus knows
what to do.
Everything
will be okay.
I don't need
to ask questions.
I don't need to know
the reason why. I am His.
He is here. Everything will
be okay.

"And in that day you will ask Me nothing."
JOHN 16:23

A Prayer

O Lord, here are my hands. Take them and make something beautiful and new. And here are my feet. Let them follow You wherever You may go.

My thoughts for Jesus

_____

_____

In Jesus' Name
May 29

Jesus' name is not a magic word that I use to get everything I want. But when I am truly His—when my heart and mind and everything I want belong to Him—I can ask God for anything. And He will do it!

"In that day you will ask in My name."
JOHN 16:26

A Prayer

O Lord, You know what this new day will bring. Thank You for all the amazing things You have planned and for working all of them out for my good.

My thoughts for Jesus

_____

_____

Yes, But. . .
May 30

I want to follow
Jesus. But what
if He asks me
to do something
crazy? What will
I do then? I will trust Him.
I will risk everything and do
what God says. When He asks
me to jump out in faith, I will
trust Him. I know He will catch me.

*"Lord,
I will follow
You, but. . ."*
LUKE 9:61

A Prayer

Thank You, Lord, for giving me a new heart. Please help the words and deeds in my own life line up with the good things I have said about You to others.

My thoughts for Jesus

_____

_____

What God Can Do

May 31

People will
hurt me. But
I won't let that
make me mad.
I know what God's
love can do. His love
can melt the coldest heart.
It can change anyone!
It can even change me.

*Jesus did not
commit Himself
to them. . .for
He knew what
was in man.*
JOHN 2:24–25

A Prayer

Thank You, Lord, for Your amazing power that has
taken this broken little body and made it healthy,
whole, healed, alive, and good as new. I love You.

My thoughts for Jesus

_____

_____

But What about Him?

June 1

But what about him? Can God save him? Can his tangled-up heart be made new? God knows! God has done it before. He did it for me. And I know God will do it again.

"Son of man, can these bones live?"
EZEKIEL 37:3

A Prayer

O Lord, You know me inside and out and You love me anyway. Please come and fill me with Your holy light. I am tired and dull and I need Your touch.

My thoughts for Jesus

_____

_____

Haunted—by God!

June 2

God wants to haunt me! He wants to fill up every attic and closet and basement in my heart until nothing else can get inside. No worries. No cares. No shadows or fears. His Spirit scared them all away. Haunt me, Jesus!

Who is the man that fears the LORD?
PSALM 25:12

A Prayer

O Lord, please come and touch me today. Fill me up with Your new life until every last little part of me is awake and alive with Your power and light.

My thoughts for Jesus

_____

_____

Secret Joy

June 3

Who is my true friend? The one who shares her hurts? Maybe. But anyone can do that. And just about anyone will. A true friend longs to share her secret joy. God's secret joy is Jesus. He shares Jesus with me. And now Jesus' secret joy *is* me.

The secret of the LORD is with those who fear Him.
PSALM 25:14

A Prayer

Thank You, Jesus, for a tender heart that longs to do Your will. What a joy it is to know You. Please show me what You want me to do and I will do it.

My thoughts for Jesus

_____

_____

Never Ever

June 4

Jesus said He would never leave me. He said He would never stop loving me. And not one of my sinful, foolish mistakes will ever make Him change His mind.

"I will never leave you nor forsake you." HEBREWS 13:5

A Prayer

O Lord, rise up again in breathtaking beauty and fill this new day and everything in it with Your mighty power and the hope and healing it brings.

My thoughts for Jesus

_____

_____

Fear Not!

June 5

God wants
me to say
what He
says. And
I can trust
everything

that God says. Am I afraid?
I will remember the Bible.
And the Bible says, *"Fear not!"*

*He Himself
has said. . .
So we may
boldly say. . .*
HEBREWS 13:5–6

A Prayer

O Jesus, please help me. I feel lost and cold and
so afraid. Touch my heart. Send Your holy fire into
the deepest, darkest part so I can sing again.

My thoughts for Jesus

_____

_____

Work It Out

June 6

I will "work out" what God has "worked in." Jesus changed my heart. But do my words and my deeds shine with the light of His love? I won't always do the right thing. And sometimes I won't even want to. But God is inside me, helping me.

Work out your own salvation.
PHILIPPIANS 2:12

A Prayer

O Lord, here is my heart. Lift me above these dark clouds and shine Your light on me so I can sparkle Your beauty all over everyone I meet today.

My thoughts for Jesus

_____

_____

My One True Love

June 7

What is the most important thing in my life? Is it a person? A thing? When I make Jesus my one true love, everything else will bloom and grow just the way it should.

"If you ask anything in My name, I will do it."
JOHN 14:14

A Prayer

Thank You, Jesus, for Your loving-kindness and for allowing me to come boldly before Your throne knowing You will hear and answer my prayers.

My thoughts for Jesus

_____

_____

Ship Ahoy!
June 8

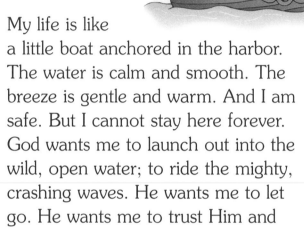

My life is like
a little boat anchored in the harbor.
The water is calm and smooth. The
breeze is gentle and warm. And I am
safe. But I cannot stay here forever.
God wants me to launch out into the
wild, open water; to ride the mighty,
crashing waves. He wants me to let
go. He wants me to trust Him and
follow Him wherever He may go.

*"If you
know these
things,
blessed are
you if you
do them."*
JOHN 13:17

A Prayer

O Lord, I want to help my friends. They need You
so much. Give me the courage to sail out of my
safe little harbor and lead them to home to You.

My thoughts for Jesus

_____

_____

Poor in Spirit
June 9

My heart
is like
a poor,
hungry
beggar.
Without Jesus
my heart is empty. But I won't
be ashamed to beg. Jesus loves
poor beggars. The kingdom of
heaven belongs to them!

*"For everyone
who asks
received."*
LUKE 11:10

A Prayer

Thank You, Lord, for our little church. Let it be a
strength to the poor, a real help to those in need,
and a shelter from the storms all around us.

My thoughts for Jesus

_____

_____

Knock, Knock!

June 10

Jesus said, "Knock and I will open the door. Ask and you will receive." But what am I asking for? Do I really need more new things? Or do I need Jesus to come into my heart— and make everything new?

"Seek, and you will find." LUKE 11:9

A Prayer

Thank You, Jesus, for coming into my heart. Thank You for making everything new. You've done so much for me in so many ways. I want to be more like You.

My thoughts for Jesus

_____

_____

Come to Me
June 11

O God, what
should I do?
I don't want
to be selfish
anymore. But
I don't know
how to stop! Did
Jesus say, "Stop"? No! Jesus said,
"Come!" I will stop trying to stop.
I will run into His arms. Look out,
Jesus. Here I come!

"Come to
Me."
MATTHEW
11:28

A Prayer
O Lord, let the gentle rain of Your Spirit fall on me
today. Soften my dried-up, dusty old heart and
make me fresh and clean and new.

My thoughts for Jesus

_____

_____

Just the Chicken Pox?

June 12

Jesus wants me to be like Him. Does all of me look like Jesus? Or am I still selfish sometimes? Am I all speckled with little selfish spots, as though I had the chicken pox? Jesus wants to heal all of me. If I follow Him, He will make me like Him.

"Rabbi. . . where are You staying?" . . . *"Come and see."* JOHN 1:38–39

A Prayer

O Lord, please help me. So many silly things are trying to climb up and sit upon Your throne. Cast them all down and be my true King once more.

My thoughts for Jesus

_____

_____

Not for Me to Say

June 13

Jesus wants me to follow Him. He wants me to act like Him. It's not my job to tell other people how they should act. I just have to follow Jesus. Then they will see Him in me.

"Follow Me."
MARK 1:17

A Prayer

O Lord, I know the plans You have for me are good. And I want to start right now. Keep me quiet on the inside so I can hear You and wait until You say go.

My thoughts for Jesus

_____

_____

It's Not about Me
June 14

I can trust God.
My heart does
not have to
be a junk
drawer full
of worries and
doubts. In every big, scary
thing—in every little, ordinary
thing—I can trust Him.
I don't have to be afraid.

"Abide in Me."
JOHN 15:4

A Prayer

O Jesus, I want to know You. Not in a small, shallow, dip-in-my-toes way. But in a big, deep, over-my-head-and-holding-my-breath way that says I am Yours.

My thoughts for Jesus

_____

_____

No Big Thing

June 15

Jesus did big
things. And
I want to do
big things, too.
But I don't need to be a star.
I can pour out God's love in
a million little ways. Jesus did
amazing miracles. But He knelt
down and washed dirty feet, as
well. I will do little loving things, too.

But also. . .
add. . .
2 PETER 1:5

A Prayer

Thank You, Lord Jesus, for gentle rain and good ground to grow in. Forgive me for being so slow to blossom into all You want me to be.

My thoughts for Jesus

_____

_____

Taste and See

June 16

My life won't
always shine.
Jesus' life
didn't shine
all the time,
either. But
He always followed God.
He was always loving.
Every day, even.

"Greater love has no one than this, than to lay down one's life for his friends."
JOHN 15:13

A Prayer

O Lord, please forgive me for thinking I deserve all the good things You do for me. Thank You for taking my sins away. I would be lost without You.

My thoughts for Jesus

_____

_____

Don't

June 17

Do I like to point out other people's faults? Jesus says, "Don't." God can do that without hurting. But I am not God. When I point out every tiny little thing that is wrong with my friend, I can be sure that there is still a great big ugly thing wrong with me.

"Judge not, that you be not judged" MATTHEW 7:1

A Prayer

O Lord, please help me see the goodness and beauty in all the people and things You've placed in my life. Thank You for being so good to me.

My thoughts for Jesus

_____

_____

Just Don't Look Down

June 18

Peter walked
on the water.
The waves
were crashing.
The wind was howling.
But Peter didn't see the waves.
He didn't feel the wind. All he
saw was Jesus. I can do anything God wants—if I will
keep my eyes on Him.

*But when he
saw that the
wind was
boisterous,
he was afraid.*
MATTHEW 14:30

A Prayer

O Lord, please help me to stop thinking so much
about myself and all the things I want. Teach me
how to put the needs of others ahead of my own.

My thoughts for Jesus

_____

_____

It's All for Ewe

June 19

Jesus wants
me to feed
His sheep.
His "sheep"
are everywhere.
I can feed them by being
kind and loving. I don't have
to make people act the way
I think they should. I just
have to love them.

*"Do you love
Me? . . .
Feed My
sheep."*
JOHN 21:17

A Prayer

O Lord, come and touch my heart and my mind
today. Fill me to overflowing with Your wisdom and
beauty so I can love and walk and think like You.

My thoughts for Jesus

_____

_____

When to Say When
June 20

I will pray for my friend. She needs to know that Jesus loves her. Jesus wants to help her. I will not wait until later. He wants me to pray for her. I will do it now. I will stop worrying so much about my own problems. I will pray.

And the LORD restored Job's losses when he prayed for his friends.
JOB 42:10

A Prayer

Thank You, Lord Jesus, for my family and friends. Teach us all to be the kind of people You can use to touch the world with Your kindness and love.

My thoughts for Jesus

_____

_____

Keep It Simple
June 21

I will stop worrying about me. I will get down on my knees. I will pray for others. I will stop thinking about me so much.

But you are. . .a royal priesthood.
1 PETER 2:9

A Prayer

O Lord, protect my heart and my mind from the lies and dreams and shadows and illusions that try to block the light of Your truth today.

My thoughts for Jesus

_____

_____

A Tough Test
June 22

My friend can be pushy and selfish. But why does it bother me? Is it because he should know better? Or because those very same things live in my heart, too? God forgives me. So I can forgive my friend.

"For with what judgment you judge, you will be judged."
MATTHEW 7:2

A Prayer

O Lord, how I need Your touch today. Please come and let the mighty wind of Your Holy Spirit blow over me until I am alive, awake, beautiful, and free.

My thoughts for Jesus

_____

_____

Jesus Rules!

June 23

Who is the king
of my heart?
Is it Jesus?
Or is it sin?
My heart cannot
not serve two kings. When
I'm selfish, I make sin the king
instead of God. I kill God's life
in me. I don't want to make God
sad. I want God to be my King.

*. . .a Man of
sorrows and
acquainted
with grief.*
ISAIAH 53:3

A Prayer

Thank You, Jesus, for changing my life. Thank You
for making my heart Your home. I never knew You
would be so good. I love You more than anything.

My thoughts for Jesus

_____

_____

It Is Sin
June 24

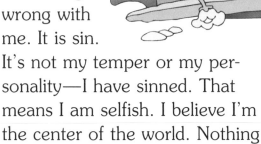

There is something wrong with me. It is sin. It's not my temper or my personality—I have sinned. That means I am selfish. I believe I'm the center of the world. Nothing can make me better—nothing but the blood of Jesus Christ.

"This is your hour, and the power of darkness." LUKE 22:53

A Prayer

O Lord, swamp me with Your kindness today. Roll me in relentless waves of goodness until I am dripping and drenched with Your great love.

My thoughts for Jesus

_____

_____

Make It Through
June 25

It's okay to cry. Bad things happen. God did not make a mistake. He did not stop loving me. He is working for my good, even though I can't understand. God is here. And we will make it through.

"What shall I say? 'Father, save Me from this hour'?"
JOHN 12:27–28

A Prayer

O Jesus, thank You for this beautiful new day and for Your gentle, loving hands that move with such great power and kindness in my life.

My thoughts for Jesus

_____

_____

New Every Morning

June 26

Jesus is ready to help me. He is ready right now. He knows what I need. He wants me to have it. His well of love will never run dry. Yesterday's help is all used up. I need Him right now. So I will go and get my bucket. I will fill my bucket from the deep well of Jesus' love. And then I will pray!

We. . .plead with you not to receive the grace of God in vain.
2 CORINTHIANS 6:1

A Prayer

O Jesus, thank You for the gift of Your amazing love. I know I don't deserve it. But You gave it just the same. Help me unwrap it and share it with joy.

My thoughts for Jesus

_____

_____

Don't Lean on That

June 27

What am
I leaning on?
Is it wobbly and
weak? Or is it
steady and strong?

When I lean on Jesus, I will
stand. But if I begin to lean on
my ways and my plans and all
of my things instead of leaning
on Jesus, my things will break!
And I will fall down.

*"I am
with you
to deliver
you," says
the LORD.*
JEREMIAH 1:8

A Prayer

O Lord, I want to know You. I want to do everything
You want me to do. Whirl me in the wind of Your
goodness and mercy. How I long to be with You.

My thoughts for Jesus

_____

_____

Gotcha!
June 28

Jesus has me. I am His! I will talk about the good things He does. I will share His Word with tender love. The Word of God will bring new life. But first it must flow clean and pure in me.

. . .lay hold of that for which Christ Jesus has also laid hold of me.
PHILIPPIANS 3:12

A Prayer

O Lord, I want to see You. I want to feel Your gentle touch. Please fill up my cup until it can't hold one more drop. I am waiting here for You.

My thoughts for Jesus

_____

_____

Cut It Off
June 29

I just can't do that anymore. I used to do it all the time. It never bothered me one bit. And my friends still do it. But now I know it breaks God's heart. It's like a black, rotten

"If your right hand causes you to sin. . ."
MATTHEW 5:30

spot on the apple of my life. And I am the apple of His eye. So I will cut off anything that makes a spot on my life's apple.

A Prayer

O Jesus, please come and touch my waiting heart with Your gentle hands. Lead me to the place where You are doing something wonderful today.

My thoughts for Jesus

_____

_____

Do It Now

June 30

Am I mad
at my friend?
Jesus says,
"Forgive!"
But I was
right and she was wrong!
It doesn't matter. Jesus
says, "Forgive her." He
says, "Make it right."
He says, "Do it now."

*"Agree with
your adversary
quickly."*
MATTHEW 5:25

A Prayer

O Lord, rush into my heart like a mighty river. Let
the wild white water of Your amazing new life flow
deep and wide in and out of my life today.

My thoughts for Jesus

_____

_____

You're under Arrest
July 1

I was wrong. Jesus asked me to forgive. But I would 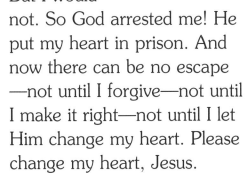 not. So God arrested me! He put my heart in prison. And now there can be no escape —not until I forgive—not until I make it right—not until I let Him change my heart. Please change my heart, Jesus.

"You will by no means get out of there till you have paid the last penny."
MATTHEW 5:26

A Prayer

O Lord, please forgive me for ignoring You when You told me what to do. Bring me back to the place where I can hear Your voice again.

My thoughts for Jesus

_____

_____

I Can't Do That
July 2

She is my very best friend. And we always do everything together! But now she wants me to do something wrong—something that will break God's heart! I love her very much. But I can't do that. My heart belongs to Him.

"If anyone comes to Me and does not hate. . . he cannot be My disciple."
LUKE 14:26

A Prayer

Thank You, Jesus, for touching my life and making everything beautiful and new. Rise up in power and shine Your holy light into my heart, mighty King.

My thoughts for Jesus

_____

_____

Put It There
July 3

O Lord, please
help me. I keep
making the same
mistake over
and over again.

I want to change. I know this
is wrong. Take my selfishness.
Burn it with the fire of Your
love. I know it will hurt. But
I want to be filled with love.

*"Woe is me, for
I am undone!
Because I am
a man of
unclean lips."*
ISAIAH 6:5

A Prayer

Thank you, Jesus, for a pure heart. Thank You for a
sound mind and the strength to control my emotions. Bless this day with the gift of Your peace.

My thoughts for Jesus

_____

_____

Don't Worry about It

July 4

Oh, silly me! There I go again, worrying about what might happen. God will work it all out. But I worry He won't work it out the way I want. I don't need to have my own way, though. When I open my heart to God's way, all my worries go away.

Do not fret— it only causes harm.
PSALM 37:8

A Prayer

O Lord, how I long to be with You. Thank You for protecting me and for saving my life. Hide me in the shadow of Your wings, mighty God.

My thoughts for Jesus

_____

_____

Count on God

July 5

I can count on God. When trouble comes, God will be with me. When good things come, He will be there, too. So when I make plans, I'll always remember —no matter what happens, God will be there.

Commit your way to the LORD. . . and He shall bring it to pass.
PSALM 37:5

A Prayer

O Jesus, please help me to be simple and small enough to hear You when You say, "You may ask Me for anything in My name, and I will do it."

My thoughts for Jesus

_____

_____

Dream Come True

July 6

I have a dream.
And God will make
that dream come
true, because my
life is His. My dreams are His,
too—His to shape and mold
into anything He wants. So
I will let God shape my dreams.
They are in good hands. He
is making something beautiful.

*The parched
ground
shall
become
a pool.*
ISAIAH 35:7

A Prayer

O Jesus, thank You for holding me safely in the palm of Your hand. Help me choose Your path and not my own. I want to be a real joy to Your heart.

My thoughts for Jesus

_____

_____

Exactly Like Him

July 7

It's not always easy to do the right thing. And thank God it's not! Following Jesus is good exercise. It makes me work hard. But Jesus is changing my heart. And He will not stop until I am exactly like Him. He loves me.

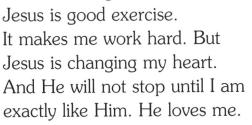

"Narrow is the gate and difficult is the way which leads to life." MATTHEW 7:14

A Prayer

O Jesus, my heart is so dark and empty without the light of Your great love. Please come and fill me to overflowing. I want to see You once again.

My thoughts for Jesus

_____

_____

I Will
July 8

I want to
follow Jesus.
But where
will He lead
me? I don't really know.
But I do know He loves
me. And He will be there,
no matter what happens.
So I won't be afraid. I will
serve the Lord!

*"Choose for
yourselves
this day
whom
you will
serve."*
JOSHUA 24:15

A Prayer

Thank you, Lord Jesus, for breaking my heart and
for picking up the broken pieces and putting them
back together in a way that is pleasing to You.

My thoughts for Jesus

_____

_____

Who, Me?

July 9

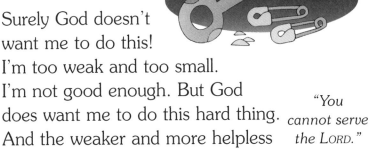

Surely God doesn't want me to do this! I'm too weak and too small. I'm not good enough. But God does want me to do this hard thing. And the weaker and more helpless I am, the better! God isn't looking for someone with something. He's looking for someone with nothing—nothing but His Son, Jesus.

"You cannot serve the LORD." JOSHUA 24:19

A Prayer

O Lord, touch me with Your beauty and loving-kindness. Bring this broken body back to life. I want to laugh and sing and jump for joy.

My thoughts for Jesus

_____

_____

Time to Wake Up
July 10

Jesus loves me. He wants me to be happy. But He doesn't want me  to be lazy. Jesus wants to stir up my sleepy heart. He wants me to get busy. He wants me to go out and share His love with my friends.

Stir up love and good works.
HEBREWS 10:24–25

A Prayer

Thank You, Jesus, for saving me from my lazy, sluggish, stagnant, lifeless, dormant, silly self and shaking me back to wild new life again.

My thoughts for Jesus

_____

_____

That I May Know Him
July 11

I want to know
Jesus. I want to
serve Him. But
I don't want to
get mixed up.
I don't want to
think that the good things I do are
more important than Jesus. I don't
want to look at the good things
I do. I just want to look at Jesus.

*. . .that
I may
know Him.*
PHILIPPIANS 3:10

A Prayer

O Lord, come and fill up my heart with the fire of
Your Holy Spirit. Twist and tangle us together
until I am everything You want me to be.

My thoughts for Jesus

_____

_____

Body Building

July 12

Jesus wants me to build up His Body. Everyone in the world who loves Jesus is part of His Body. Jesus' Body needs me to do my part. I need to care about others, not just myself. Then I will be a Body builder!

. . .till we all come. . .to the measure of the stature of the fullness of Christ.
EPHESIANS 4:13

A Prayer

O Lord, You are so big and so amazing my mind can hardly take it in. Thank You for this life and for making me a part of Your family. I love You, mighty King.

My thoughts for Jesus

_____

_____

Good-bye, Old Friend

July 13

My friend moved away. I had to say good-bye to him. Oh, how I miss him. My heart feels empty without him. But now I have more room in my heart for Jesus. Jesus will fill the empty space with His love.

In the year that King Uzziah died, I saw the Lord.
ISAIAH 6:1

A Prayer

Thank You, Jesus, for the joy that comes from knowing You are alive and well and coming soon. Let me live this day in a way that pleases You.

My thoughts for Jesus

_____

_____

Coward!

July 14

He hurt me. And now I want to hurt him back! But I must not. That would hurt Jesus. I am not a coward. I am someone who follows Jesus. So I will forgive. And I will turn the other cheek.

"But whoever slaps you on your right cheek, turn the other to him also."
MATTHEW 5:39

A Prayer

O Lord, here is my heart. All I ever really wanted was for You to take my life and make all of Your hopes and dreams for me come true.

My thoughts for Jesus

_____

_____

IOU

July 15

I owe everything to Jesus. So I will let Him change my heart. I will let Him pour His love out through me. Here I am, Lord. Take me where You will. My heart belongs to You.

I am a debtor both to Greeks and to barbarians.
ROMANS 1:14

A Prayer

O Lord, if there is anything I put in my mind or my hand or my mouth that breaks Your heart, please show me so I can put those things away for good.

My thoughts for Jesus

_____

_____

He Won't Forget

July 16

I'm not sure what to do. But I'm not going to worry about it. Why should I worry? God is my Father. He loves me. I won't ever think of anything that He will forget!

"How much more will your Father. . .give good things to those who ask Him!"
MATTHEW 7:11

A Prayer

Thank You, Jesus, for filling this new day with the warmth and beauty of Your kindness and love. Touch me with power today. I want to be like You.

My thoughts for Jesus

_____

_____

I Can't See You!

July 17

Do I want people to like me? Do I want them to see how good I am? That seems like a good thing. But when people look at me—they can't see Jesus. The cure for this problem is very simple. Jesus wants me to give up trying to impress everyone. Right now.

When I came to you, [I] did not come with excellence of speech or of wisdom.
1 CORINTHIANS 2:1

A Prayer

O Lord, I need You so much. Wash me in the wild white water of Your Holy Spirit until my thoughts and my words are clean and pure once again.

My thoughts for Jesus

_____

_____

My Master

July 18

Many people would like to tell me what to do. They would like to see me do things that would break God's heart. But I will not listen to them. And I don't have to! My heart listens to only one Person. And His name is Jesus Christ.

And he said, "Who are You, Lord?" Acts 9:5

A Prayer

O Lord, so many homeless, hopeless moods are wandering around in my heart just now. Please light up this darkness so I can find my way back to You.

My thoughts for Jesus

_____

_____

You Are Worthy

July 19

God will not force me to obey. If He did, He would be like a mean teacher who didn't care about me. But when I see God for who He is—when I feel His love in my heart—what can I say but "Yes, Lord, I will do whatever You say"?

"You call Me Teacher and Lord, and you say well, for so I am."
JOHN 13:13

A Prayer

Thank You, Jesus, for drawing me close and holding me still in Your mighty arms. Help me to stop and stay in the place where You can bless and use me.

My thoughts for Jesus

_____

_____

Treasure

July 20

There are times
when God will
do amazing
things. And
that is very exciting.
But I must never allow
the excitement of what
God can do steal away
the treasure of who
He is. He loves me!

*Those who wait
on the L<small>ORD</small>. . .shall
walk and not faint.*
I<small>SAIAH</small> 40:31

A Prayer

O Jesus, please help me. I am completely, totally,
utterly, absolutely, unspeakably wonderfully lost
and altogether hopelessly in love with You.

My thoughts for Jesus

_____

_____

Blessed Like This

July 21

I've tried so hard to be good. I've tried to do what Jesus says. But I just can't do it! Is God mad at me? No! *I have been blessed!* Jesus says, "Stop trying to be good. Let Me come inside. Now I can change your heart."

"Blessed are the poor in spirit." MATTHEW 5:3

A Prayer

O Lord, please help me clear away the junk that has piled up in the space between us so I can see You clearly and know what You want me to do.

My thoughts for Jesus

_____

_____

Saints and Children
July 22

I am a good friend. I like to help. My parents are proud of me. I want to grow up to be someone special. And that's good. But God wants something different. He wants me! He wants to make my heart His home.

This is the will of God, your sanctification.
1 THESSALONIANS 4:3

A Prayer

O Lord, please teach me to stop sipping at Your goodness when I'm in the right mood and to allow myself to be drawn completely into Your heart.

My thoughts for Jesus

_____

_____

It's Mine

July 23

Everything God has is mine. His goodness. His love. His holiness. His faith. Everything! He gave them all to me. Because I deserve it? No. Because He loves me.

. . .wisdom. . .and righteousness and sanctification and redemption.
1 CORINTHIANS 1:30

A Prayer

O Lord, I know all I care to know about the bad thoughts that live in my heart and in the hearts of my friends. I want to know what is in Your heart.

My thoughts for Jesus

_____

_____

To Be or Not to Be

July 24

Jesus wants me to do the right thing. But He wants me to *be* the right thing even more. God sees all the good things I do. But why do I do them? Jesus wants my reasons to be as clean and pure as He is.

"Unless your righteousness exceeds the righteousness of the scribes. . ."
MATTHEW 5:20

A Prayer

O Jesus, I know You are leading me. But I just can't seem to see where we are going. Lift me up into the light. I want to do what You want me to do.

My thoughts for Jesus

_____

_____

Dynamite
July 25

God's Word is like dynamite! It will explode everything in my heart that was not built by Jesus. I don't always understand God's Word. But when I am still— and when I listen with my heart— *kaboom!* God's Spirit blows away the darkness and I can see.

"Blessed are. . ."
MATTHEW 5:3

A Prayer

O Lord, teach me to pray great big mountain-sized prayers whose peaks will rip the darkest clouds in two and allow Your light to explode into my life.

My thoughts for Jesus

_____

_____

Pure in Heart

July 26

God knows
my heart. He
knows about
the good things
that live there. He knows
about the bad things, too.
I don't have to pretend there
are no bad things. God can
fix the bad things. But first
I must give Him my heart.

*"Out of
the heart
proceed. . ."*
MATTHEW 15:19

A Prayer

O Jesus, I am so quick to be angry and critical of
others. Please burn away the trash that has piled
up in my heart with the fire of Your Holy Spirit.

My thoughts for Jesus

_____

_____

The Way to Know
July 27

Do I want to know
what the Bible means?
Then I must do what
the Bible says. Do I feel
a little confused about what
God wants? Then there must be
something I don't want to obey!
Maybe I don't want to share.
Maybe I don't want to forgive
someone. If I let Him, God's
Spirit will show me what to do.

"If anyone wills to do His will, he shall know concerning the doctrine."
JOHN 7:17

A Prayer

O Lord, I have been waiting so long. Where have You gone? Why are You hiding? Please let me know if I'm on the right path. I am lost without You.

My thoughts for Jesus

_____

_____

What Is God's Goal?
July 28

I did just what God said. And now He has to make me a big success. Right? Maybe. But God's goal is not my success. That is my goal. God's goal is that I trust Him and treat peple right as I try to do His will.

He made His disciples get into the boat and go before Him to the other side.
MARK 6:45

A Prayer

O Lord, I don't understand why this is happening. But I know You love me and You will work it all out for my good. So I will thank You, and I will rejoice.

My thoughts for Jesus

_____

_____

They Came with Him!

July 29

The sky is dark with angry clouds. Did God go away? No! *The clouds are a sign that He is here.* Without them I would have no faith—no faith that God can blow clouds away. And when He does, clean bright light will shine in my heart.

Behold, He is coming with clouds.
REVELATION 1:7

A Prayer

Jesus, these clouds are nothing more than the dust around Your feet. I can find You and Your loving-kindness in each one. There is nothing to fear.

My thoughts for Jesus

_____

_____

Just an Illusion
July 30

I thought she would help. I thought she cared. She was my one true friend. How could she do that to me? At first I was hurt. But now I see. God doesn't want me to give my heart to anyone but Jesus. And when my heart belongs to Him, no one else can hurt me.

Jesus did not commit Himself to them. . .for He knew what was in man.
JOHN 2:24–25

A Prayer

O Lord, I don't really know what You are going to do. And I have no earthly idea how You will do it. But I do know this: Whatever it is, it will be amazing.

My thoughts for Jesus

_____

_____

Sloppy Joe
July 31

Jesus loves me—mistakes and all. But He is not about to leave me that way! God says,
"Tuck those in! Button that up!" He will finish what He started. And my heart will be beautiful.

Let patience have its perfect work.
JAMES 1:4

A Prayer

O Lord, let the sight and the sound of Your glory and beauty sweep over me until I am caught up and lost in the music of Your amazing love.

My thoughts for Jesus

_____

_____

Did I Go?

August 1

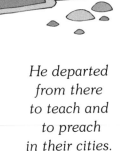

God said, "Go." But did I go? Or did I worry about myself? My friend needs to know about Jesus. I will not keep God's love locked up inside. I will give it all away. I will go.

He departed from there to teach and to preach in their cities.
MATTHEW 11:1

A Prayer

O Lord, thank You for giving me the courage to walk steadily along the path You have chosen for me so I can know for sure I have done the right thing.

My thoughts for Jesus

_____

_____

Strength!

August 2

Trouble will come. But I am not afraid. God is bigger than any trouble. I can turn and face my fear.

I can look it in the eye. Jesus says, "Stand and fight." Where has my fear gone? When I gave it to Jesus, it turned into something else. The thing that used to make me weak now makes me strong.

"Be of good cheer, I have overcome the world."
John 16:33

A Prayer

O Lord, You are so big. And I am so small. Please lift me up out of the pit of my own weakness and fear. I want to be alive, clean, and in step with You again.

My thoughts for Jesus

_____

_____

Big God
August 3

God picked me. He has a plan for my life. We will go many places. Together we will do wonderful things. But His plan is much bigger than places or things. I cannot see it just now. But in my heart I hear it calling. I hear it calling me to Him!

"Behold, we are going up to Jerusalem."
LUKE 18:31

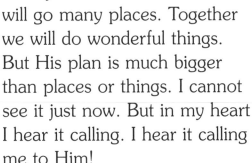

A Prayer

Thank You, Jesus, for lifting me, leading me, and filling me with the joy that makes my heart sing Your beautiful love song to everyone I meet.

My thoughts for Jesus

_____

_____

Brave God
August 4

Who can God use? That's easy. God can use anyone— anyone who puts God first. My friendship with God is the most important thing in my life.

Then He took the twelve aside.
LUKE 18:31

A Prayer

O Lord, there are so many things that would love to make me trip and fall away from Your side. But I will not be led astray. The only thing I want is You.

My thoughts for Jesus

_____

_____

What Is God Doing?

August 5

Why did this happen? What is God doing? I don't know. But God knows. And I can relax and trust Him. God sees what I do not. He is using this to make something beautiful.

But they understood none of these things.
LUKE 18:34

A Prayer

O Jesus, please forgive me. I have become so tied up and tangled in trying to be good that I have forgotten You love me just the way I am.

My thoughts for Jesus

_____

_____

Why to Pray

August 6

God knows
my heart.
He knows
just what
I need. Before
I even think to ask, His answer
is already on the way. Jesus longs
to hear my voice. Jesus died to
set me free. Oh, how He loves
me. I will talk to Him.

"In that day you will ask in My name."
JOHN 16:26

A Prayer

O Lord, please forgive me for acting like I know
it all when I can't even measure the full length
of my own sin.

My thoughts for Jesus

_____

_____

In My Father's House

August 7

I want to live in my Father's house. I want to curl up in His arms. I want His heart to beat in mine. I want to listen to His gentle voice. O Lord, have Your way with me.

"Did you not know that I must be about My Father's business?"
LUKE 2:49

A Prayer

O Lord, I have wandered far away from You. Please wash away the sin that has stained my life so I can crawl up in Your lap and hold You close once more.

My thoughts for Jesus

_____

_____

Room for Him

August 8

God put His Son in me. And now Jesus is born again inside my heart. He will live there. He will grow there. When Mary gave birth to the baby Jesus, there was no room for Him in the inn. But this time there is plenty of room for His Spirit—right here in my heart!

"That Holy One who is to be born will be called the Son of God." LUKE 1:35

A Prayer

O Jesus, come plant the seed of Your truth in my heart. Teach me to draw my life from Your Word so I can bloom with all the beautiful colors of Your love.

My thoughts for Jesus

_____

_____

Simply Beautiful

August 9

Does God hear me when I pray? Of course He does! God will always hear the prayers of His Son. And His Son is alive and well—right here inside of my heart!

"Father, I thank You that You have heard Me."
JOHN 11:41

A Prayer

Thank You, Jesus, for the love that is making me like a tree planted by the water—strong and tall with branches full of good fruit at just the right time.

My thoughts for Jesus

_____

_____

Nobody Knows
August 10

My friend is
hurting. I want
to help her.
I just don't know
what to say or do.

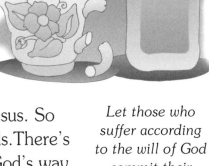

I know she loves Jesus. So
she is in good hands. There's
no need to get in God's way.
I will pray. Jesus will heal
her broken heart.

*Let those who
suffer according
to the will of God
commit their
souls to Him.*
1 PETER 4:19

A Prayer

O Lord, how I thank You for the terrible, lonely
feeling that forced me to wander through the
desert in desperate circles until I finally found You.

My thoughts for Jesus

_____

_____

This Must Come

August 11

I feel so lonely. I miss my old friend. Everywhere I go, I remember the things we used to do together. I can't stop thinking about my friend. But God wants me to think about Him. My friend trusted God. And I will, too.

So he saw him no more.
2 KINGS 2:12

Rest
August 12

Did I hear the howling wind? Did I see the crashing waves? Did I feel the angry, rolling sea? No, I'm sorry. I must have missed it. I was here with Jesus. All I could see was Him.

"Why are you fearful, O you of little faith?"
MATTHEW 8:26

A Prayer

Thank You, Jesus, for the simple joy of trusting in You. You've made me alive and light and free. And now at last I can laugh and sing and jump for joy.

My thoughts for Jesus

_____

_____

Quiet Now

August 13

God's voice is gentle and still. And I must be quiet to hear it. Is God saying, "Stop"? Then I will stop. God does not have to shout. I am listening to Him.

Do not quench the Spirit.

1 THESSALONIANS 5:19

A Prayer

O Lord, here is my heart. I give it freely to You. Fill me with Your Spirit. Let Your holy light rise in and all around me so I can bring real joy to Your heart.

My thoughts for Jesus

_____

_____

Let Him
August 14

Jesus loves me. And
because He does,
He will correct
me when I am
wrong. But
I don't like to
be corrected. I know
God can make me into
something beautiful. Do I love
Him enough to let Him do it?

*"Do not despise
the chastening
of the LORD."*
HEBREWS 12:5

A Prayer

O Lord, help me see beyond the faults and mistakes
of the people around me. Let me focus instead on
knowing and seeing and following You.

My thoughts for Jesus

_____

_____

Born Again

August 15

Who can be
born again?
I can! I can
stop pretending
that I am good.
I can put away my sin and
selfishness. Now Jesus can
come in. Now His love can
make my heart brand new.

"You must be born again."
JOHN 3:7

A Prayer

O Lord, I feel Your gentle hands moving upon my
heart. But what is it that You want? Show me the
way and I will follow. I am waiting here for You.

My thoughts for Jesus

_____

_____

Do I Know Him?

August 16

Do I ever wonder if Jesus can really do what people say He can? Do I doubt Him?
Do I do what I want—or do I do what Jesus wants? All my doubts and selfish feelings will go away when I'm really friends with Jesus.

"He calls his own sheep by name."
JOHN 10:3

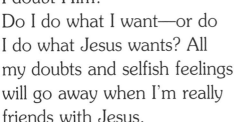

A Prayer

Thank You, Jesus, for taking this day and filling it forever with beautiful memories of Your everlasting kindness and love for me.

My thoughts for Jesus

_____

_____

Hard
August 17

Did Jesus ask
me to do some-
thing hard? Does
He want me to do what
I don't want to do? Now God
is searching my heart. He is
making it clean and pure. He
will not force me to do what
He wants. But if I love Him,
I will do what He wants me to do.

*"Sell all that
you have. . .
and come,
follow Me."*
LUKE 18:22

A Prayer

Thank You, Lord, for making this new day alive and
bright and full of Your love. Take away the sadness
and moodiness that cloud my sight of You.

My thoughts for Jesus

_____

_____

But How?
August 18

How can I do it? It's just too hard. Surely God doesn't want me to do that! But I am His. And everything I have is His, too. I will let Him shape me and use me any way He wants.

But when he heard this, he became very sorrowful, for he was very rich.
LUKE 18:23

A Prayer

O Lord, take this little house and light it up so bright that every door and window bursts forth with the glorious dawn of Your amazing love.

My thoughts for Jesus

_____

_____

Straight to Jesus

August 19

God wants me
to be whole and
healthy in Jesus.
Nothing should
upset my friendship
with Him. If anything comes
between Him and me, I need
to take care of it right away.
Then I can go straight to Jesus.

*"Come
to Me."*
MATTHEW 11:28

A Prayer

O Lord, how I thank You for filling me to overflowing
with the deep water of Your love and forgiveness
that nothing and no one can ever take away.

My thoughts for Jesus

_____

_____

Peace—Be Still!

August 20

Has something come between Jesus and me? Is it making me wobble and worry and fret? I will tell God all about it. He will blow it far away. He will put Jesus in its place.

"And I will give you rest."
MATTHEW 11:28

A Prayer

O Jesus, please help me. I am getting on my own last nerve. Please save me from my mixed-up, silly self and draw me ever deeper into Your arms.

My thoughts for Jesus

_____

_____

Poor in Spirit
August 21

Jesus loves me. I don't have to be strong or beautiful. I don't have to be important or useful or wise. I don't have to be anything at all. Here I am, Lord. Oh, how I love You.

"Blessed are the poor in spirit."
MATTHEW 5:3

A Prayer

O Lord, how I thank You that I can find and know and do exactly what You want me to do. Take my life and make it everything You want it to be.

My thoughts for Jesus

_____

_____

Good, Better, Best

August 22

Have I come to the end of my rope? Good! Am I just about ready to lose my grip? Even better! Did I let go and fall down? Best of all! At last I am lying at Jesus' feet. Now He can change my heart. He will fill me with the Holy Spirit.

He will baptize you with the Holy Spirit and fire."
MATTHEW 3:11

A Prayer

O Lord, please help! Fear is lurking in every room. And my basement is crawling with worry and doubt. Come and sweep me clean again. I am lost without Your love.

My thoughts for Jesus

_____

_____

The Secret Place

August 23

Where is my secret place—the place where God can touch my heart—the place where we can be alone? That is where Jesus wants me to live. I will run to meet Him there.

"Pray to your Father who is in the secret place."
MATTHEW 6:6

A Prayer

O Lord, how I love to spend these quiet morning hours with You. Please let Your beautiful peace spill over into every moment of this busy day.

My thoughts for Jesus

_____

_____

I Forgot
August 24

Did God forget to answer my prayer? Or did I forget how to be loving and kind? I will ask God to forgive me. I will ask my friends to forgive me, too. Now when I pray, I know God will answer.

"What man. . .if his son asks for bread, will give him a stone?"
MATTHEW 7:9

A Prayer

O Lord, when I think of all You've done for me, I can't help but fall down at Your feet and give You praise. Thank You for taking such good care of me.

My thoughts for Jesus

_____

_____

Friends
August 25

Here is my
heart, Lord.
And here is
my life, too.
Please teach
me how to love.
Let me long to do Your
will. Oh, how I love You.
You are my friend.

*"I have called
you friends."*
JOHN 15:15

A Prayer

O Lord, let this little house ring with the gladness
and joy that have given me new life, a fresh start,
and the freedom to be all You want me to be.

My thoughts for Jesus

_____

_____

Am I Rubbing Him Out?

August 26

Do I worry and fret over every little thing? Worry is like an eraser. It rubs out God's face until I can't even see Him anymore. I will stop rubbing God out. God is not worried. I will trust Him. I will look up!

"Peace I leave with you, My peace I give to you."
JOHN 14:27

A Prayer

Thank You, Jesus, for this wonderful peace—deep and dark as the unmeasured ocean, quiet and still like the song of the stars. Let me fall forever into Your arms.

My thoughts for Jesus

_____

_____

Make It Real

August 27

Did God show me what to do? Then I will do it! Did He tell me to forgive? Did He ask me to share His love? Did He show me the way to go? I will do it. I will make it real.

"Walk while you have the light, lest darkness overtake you."
JOHN 12:35

A Prayer

Thank You, Jesus, for coming into my heart. Send my roots deep into the good ground of Your Word to draw power and strength from Your river of life.

My thoughts for Jesus

_____

_____

Teach Me to Pray

August 28

Why should
I pray? Should
I pray to get
things? Should
I pray to change
things? Yes, I should!
But what will I get? And what
will God change? That's easy!
I will get Jesus. And God will
change me!

"Lord, teach us to pray."
LUKE 11:1

A Prayer

O Lord, You spoke and the stars lit the sky. Every
night they come and bow before Your throne. There
is no reason to worry. Everything will be all right.

My thoughts for Jesus

_____

_____

Now It Is Mine

August 29

Do I trust God?
Then He will
test my faith.
Can I believe
Him when everything
I see and hear tells me He
is wrong? That is the test.
Jesus says, "Trust Me and
do not be afraid." When
I trust Him, faith is mine!

*"Did I not
say to you that
if you would
believe you
would see the
glory of God?"*
JOHN 11:40

A Prayer

O Lord, forgive me for being so slow to say thank You for all the good things You do for me. Give me a grateful new heart. I want to be a real joy to You.

My thoughts for Jesus

_____

_____

Wanted!

August 30

Did God use me? Good! I will thank Him. But I must never forget that God can use anyone. He can use a donkey. He can use a king! What really matters is that Jesus wants me. He loves me!

"Rejoice because your names are written in heaven." LUKE 10:20

A Prayer

O Lord, You are a treasure beyond compare. Forgive me for putting so many things ahead of You. Everything I will ever need is right here in Your hand.

My thoughts for Jesus

_____

_____

Joy!
August 31

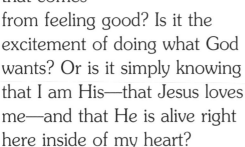

What is joy?
Is it the
happiness
that comes
from feeling good? Is it the
excitement of doing what God
wants? Or is it simply knowing
that I am His—that Jesus loves
me—and that He is alive right
here inside of my heart?

". . .that My joy may remain in you, and that your joy may be full."
JOHN 15:11

A Prayer

Thank You, Jesus, for the joy that comes from knowing You are God. Give me a quiet heart that longs to be with You more than anything else in the world.

My thoughts for Jesus

_____

_____

Holy
September 1

I am God's.
My feet will
follow where
He leads. My
lips will speak
His words of life. My thoughts
will flow clean, clear, and pure.
Search my heart, Lord. Burn
up the things that make You
sad. I want to be like You.

*"Be holy,
for I am
holy."*
1 PETER 1:16

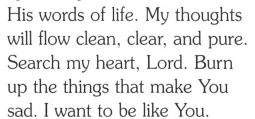

A Prayer

Thank You, Jesus, for the loving-kindness that is
changing me from the inside out. Please come and
make me everything You ever wanted me to be.

My thoughts for Jesus

_____

_____

Open Up!

September 2

God doesn't care how good I act on the outside. He doesn't care how many nice things I have. He just wants me to be like Jesus. He doesn't want me to keep my life closed up like a bottle with the top on. He wants me to take the top off and pour myself out. He wants me to share myself.

"He who believes in Me. . .out of his heart will flow rivers of living water." JOHN 7:38

A Prayer

O Lord, please fill up my life with Your goodness and love so the things I say and do bring joy to Your heart and light to everyone around me.

My thoughts for Jesus

_____

_____

Pour It Out

September 3

Did God give me something good? If I keep it all to myself, it will turn sour. But if I pour it out as a gift to others, it will be as sweet to my friend as it was to me!

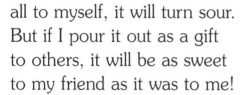

He would not drink it, but poured it out to the LORD.
2 SAMUEL 23:16

A Prayer

O Jesus, please forgive me for keeping Your love all bottled up inside. Come and wash away my sin. I want to be clean again.

My thoughts for Jesus

_____

_____

His!
September 4

Who do I belong to? Do I belong to my mother? My father? My friends? Myself? Those people love me very much. And I love them. But my heart belongs to Jesus.

"They were Yours, You gave them to Me."
JOHN 17:6

A Prayer

O Lord, please open up my eyes and ears to the beauty all around me. I want to see and hear and smell and taste just how wonderful You really are.

My thoughts for Jesus

_____

_____

In the Garden
September 5

When I was in trouble, Jesus came into the garden of my heart. He stayed with me until the terrible storm was past. Now Jesus wants me to come into the garden of His heart. He wants me to kneel down beside Him. We will pray together for my friends.

"Watch with Me." MATTHEW 26:40

A Prayer

Thank You, Lord, for the mighty hands that hold and protect me. And thank You for the gentle hands that never fail to show me the right way to go.

My thoughts for Jesus

_____

_____

Love Like a River

September 6

God's love is like a mighty river. Is there something in its way? God's love will flow right around it—or wash it clean away!

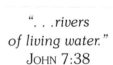

"...rivers
of living water."
JOHN 7:38

A Prayer

Thank You, Jesus, for a heart that is bold and strong. I don't ever have to be afraid. You are God Almighty. And You are fighting for me right now.

My thoughts for Jesus

_____

_____

Pull Out the Plug

September 7

Is God's river of love flowing out of me? Or am I all plugged up? I will pull out the plug! I will give God my heart. I am not a cold, dead sea whose water can't flow out. I am a river of life—a river of God's life!

"The water that I shall give him will become in him a fountain of water."
JOHN 4:14

A Prayer

Thank You, Jesus, for this beautiful new day. There is nothing in the whole wide world I would rather do than spend it here together with You.

My thoughts for Jesus

_____

_____

All the Pieces

September 8

Jesus is alive inside
my heart. And His love
washed all my sins away. But
something is wrong. My heart
longs to hate when I have been
hurt. I don't want to love someone so different from me. Did
Jesus forget to fix these things? No! He wants
me to leave them with Him. I have to give
Him the parts of me that hate. I can't keep
these things anymore. I have to let them go.

*. . .casting
down...
every high
thing that
exalts itself.*
2 CORINTHIANS 10:5

A Prayer

O Lord, thank You for the wild white waves of joy
that are flooding over my heart on this beautiful
day. Wash me inside and out. I want to be like You.

My thoughts for Jesus

_____

_____

I Will!
September 9

I want to
do many
good things
for God. But
I want to obey
Him most of all.
Did I think of something
good to do? I will tell God
about it. And if He says,
"Do it"—I will!

*. . .bringing
every thought
into captivity to
the obedience
of Christ.*
2 CORINTHIANS 10:5

A Prayer

Thank You, Jesus, for filling my life with the music of Your peace. Tune up my heart so I am in perfect harmony with You. Make this a day fit for a king.

My thoughts for Jesus

_____

_____

Out in the Open

September 10

Do I spend time alone with God? Do I tell Him how I feel inside? Do I listen for His gentle voice? If I know Him here—in the quiet, secret place—then my heart will be quiet and happy even when noisy people are all around me.

"When you were under the fig tree, I saw you."
JOHN 1:48

A Prayer

O Lord, I just don't know what to do. One day I'm up. The next day I'm down. Thank You for loving me so very much, no matter how mixed up I feel today.

My thoughts for Jesus

_____

_____

Sweet Feet
September 11

Where did God put me? What does He want me to do? Do I see a dirty foot? I will fill a bowl with water. I will go and find a towel. I will wash it nice and fresh and clean. I will do little, loving things for Jesus.

"You also ought to wash one another's feet."
JOHN 13:14

A Prayer

O mighty King, here is my heart. Come reign and rule over this grateful little kingdom that it may shine with the power and glory of Your holy name.

My thoughts for Jesus

_____

_____

Confused?

September 12

I don't understand why this is happening. And I'm not sure what to do. But I know that Jesus loves me. He is teaching me to trust Him. And the only way out of this mess is to go through it with Him.

"You do not know what you ask."
MATTHEW 20:22

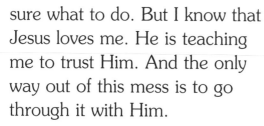

A Prayer

O Lord, please help me. I'm tired and confused and grayer than a bowl of leftover oatmeal. Please fill me with Your light so I can share Your warm love today.

My thoughts for Jesus

_____

_____

I Surrender!
September 13

Jesus wants my heart. He wants it for His very own. He will not force me to give it to Him. He will never bargain or beg. Jesus is waiting. Will I give Him my heart?

"I have finished the work which You have given Me to do."
JOHN 17:4

A Prayer

O Lord, please forgive me. I have been busy and distracted by so many silly things. Draw me back into Your heart. I want to be with You again.

My thoughts for Jesus

_____

_____

A Muddle Puddle

September 14

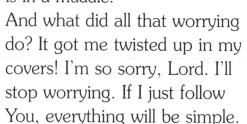

My heart is so confused I can't sleep at night. My poor mind is in a muddle! And what did all that worrying do? It got me twisted up in my covers! I'm so sorry, Lord. I'll stop worrying. If I just follow You, everything will be simple.

. . .the simplicity that is in Christ.
2 CORINTHIANS 11:3

A Prayer

O Lord, save me from the shadows that lurk in the darkness of my heart. Please come and rescue this troubled little house and fill it with Your holy light.

My thoughts for Jesus

_____

_____

Into the Light

September 15

Am I angry
with my
friend?
I will drag
that dark,
angry feeling
out into God's light. God
will chase it far away. Now
my heart is clean and pure.

*We have renounced
the hidden things
of shame.*
2 CORINTHIANS 4:2

A Prayer

O Lord, thank You for watching over the deepest
part of my heart. Keep it free from the rust that
comes so quickly when I forget to make time for You.

My thoughts for Jesus

_____

_____

Why God Hears

September 16

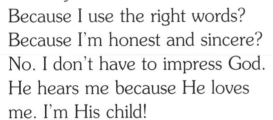

Does Jesus hear me when I pray? You bet He does! But why? Because I use the right words? Because I'm honest and sincere? No. I don't have to impress God. He hears me because He loves me. I'm His child!

"Pray to your Father who is in the secret place." MATTHEW 6:6

A Prayer

O Lord, let my heart forever shout Your word, "Be bold and strong! Banish fear and doubt! The Lord your God is with you wherever you go."

My thoughts for Jesus

_____

_____

That's Very Tempting

September 17

I'm not bad if I want
to do something
wrong. Everyone
wants to do
wrong things
sometimes. But God helps
me not to do the wrong thing.
He wants me to lean on Him
when I'm tempted to do wrong.
I will do right if I turn away
from wrong and turn to God.

*No temptation
has overtaken
you except such
as is common
to man.*
1 CORINTHIANS 10:13

A Prayer

O Lord, I am buried so deep inside this mountain
of fear and doubt I can't see or hear You anymore.
Please help me find my way back out into the light.

My thoughts for Jesus

_____

_____

So Watch Out!

September 18

Satan will tempt me. He wants me to sin. Friends may want me to do bad things. But Satan wants something much worse than that! He wants me to stop loving and caring. He wants me to lose my friendship with Jesus.

We do not have a High Priest who cannot sympathize with our weaknesses.
HEBREWS 4:15

A Prayer

O Jesus, some days I feel like I don't know You at all. Draw me close to Your heart and surround me with Your love until I speak and live only for You.

My thoughts for Jesus

_____

_____

Slip and Fall
September 19

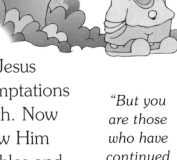

I want to follow Jesus. But sometimes He leads me through hard things. Jesus faced troubles and temptations when He was on earth. Now He wants me to follow Him through my own troubles and temptations. If I follow Him, I won't slip and fall.

"But you are those who have continued with Me in My trials."
LUKE 22:28

A Prayer

O Lord, how I thank You for another beautiful, quiet morning here in Your arms. Our time together is worth more than a million mountains of pure gold.

My thoughts for Jesus

_____

_____

It's You I Like
September 20

Some people I like. And some I do not! I won't always like everyone I meet. But if my heart truly belongs to Jesus—if I'm walking in His light—He will show me how to love people—whether I like them or not!

"You shall be perfect, just as your Father in heaven is perfect."
MATTHEW 5:48

A Prayer

O Jesus, as this new day unfolds, let Your heart be the treasure I seek and Your love and kindness the fragrance that fills the air all around me.

My thoughts for Jesus

_____

_____

Forever
September 21

Who am
I? Why am
I here? That's
easy! I am
God's. God
made me.
And I am free.
Free to worship Him and
enjoy His love—forever!

*"And now the LORD
says, Who formed
Me from the womb
to be His Servant."*
ISAIAH 49:5

A Prayer

O Lord, please come and fill me once again with Your
mighty power so I can blossom and grow here in
the good ground where You have planted me.

My thoughts for Jesus

_____

_____

Yes, Master

September 22

Jesus will never
force me to obey.
Some days I wish
He would. And some days
I wish He'd just leave me
alone. But God loves me too
much to ever do that. He
is teaching me to listen. He
is teaching me to trust Him.
He is teaching me to love.

*"You call
Me Teacher
and Lord,
and you
say well,
for so I am."*
JOHN 13:13

A Prayer

O Lord, the darkness of this world has left me
feeling hungry and dry. But I refuse to lay down
and die. I will rise up and worship You.

My thoughts for Jesus

_____

_____

Growing Up

September 23

What do
I want to
be when
I grow up?
I'm not really
sure. But I do
know this: My plans may
change. My dreams may
change, too. But no matter
what—I want to be God's.

*"Behold, we
are going up
to Jerusalem."*
LUKE 18:31

A Prayer

Thank You, Lord, for slowing me down and for
smoothing out the bumps in the road ahead.
How can I fall when my life is in Your hands?

My thoughts for Jesus

_____

_____

Get Ready

September 24

God will
use me.
But how
do I get ready?
I must let Jesus search my
heart. Did He find something
I have been hiding? I will
confess my secret sin. I will
give it all to Him. Every day
I will give Jesus my heart.

*"First be reconciled
to your brother,
and then come
and offer your gift."*
MATTHEW 5:24

A Prayer

O Lord, please release me from the weight of the
things that are trying to squeeze You out of my life
so my heart can leap and dance and sing for joy.

My thoughts for Jesus

_____

_____

So Can I
September 25

Jesus wants
me to do the
impossible.
Did some-
one hurt
my feelings?

Jesus says, "Forgive and then
forget it ever happened." But
that's impossible! That's right!
But He will forget and
forgive—and so can I.

*"Whoever com-
pels you to go
one mile,
go with him
two."*
MATTHEW 5:41

A Prayer

Thank You, Jesus, for the prayers of my family and
friends that have surrounded me like a beautiful
summer day and lifted my heart back up to You.

My thoughts for Jesus

_____

_____

Go Back
September 26

I am mad at her.
And she is mad
at me. Now I want
to sing and give thanks to God.
But Jesus says, "No." He says
first I must forgive. But why me?
That's easy! Jesus wants every
last little part of me to be just
like Him. So I must go back
and make things right with her.

*"If you. . .
remember
that your
brother has
something
against
you. . ."*
MATTHEW 5:23

A Prayer

O Lord, You are good. Your wisdom and power go
on forever. Thank You for the love I do not deserve.
Here is my heart. Have Your way with me.

My thoughts for Jesus

_____

_____

Peace and Joy
September 27

I love the Bible. It brings peace and joy. But sometimes it can hurt. Did  God's Word find something in my heart that has to go? God loves me, but He wants to make me like Jesus. His love will shine on all my selfish darkness.

"Lord, I will follow You wherever You go."
LUKE 9:57

A Prayer

O Jesus, it is so hard to say good-bye. But deep in my heart I know this is not the end. These beautiful memories will be my treasure until we meet again.

My thoughts for Jesus

_____

_____

Here's Looking at You
September 28

Jesus looked at me. He looked right into my heart! He saw my mistakes. He saw all my fears. He crumpled them up. He threw them all away. Now I can see Him! Oh, how He loves me. Now at last my heart is free!

"One thing you lack. . .come, take up the cross, and follow Me."
MARK 10:21

A Prayer

O Lord, my heart feels so empty. I want to speak. But I don't know what to say. Quiet. Quiet! Peace. Be still. Everything will be all right. Jesus is here.

My thoughts for Jesus

_____

_____

God Calling!

September 29

God has a plan for me. I don't know what it is right now. I don't know what I'll see or do.  But one day I will hear Him call. And when I do, if I will answer yes, Jesus will do something amazing!

Woe is me if I do not preach the gospel!
1 CORINTHIANS 9:16

A Prayer

O Lord, thank You for new life, for a fresh start, and for Your power, fitness, and heavenly health in and through everything I say and do today.

My thoughts for Jesus

_____

_____

Bread and Wine

September 30

God wants to use me
to help others. He
wants to put His love inside me—
and then He wants me to pour
it out to my friends and family.
When people have hungry hearts,
He wants my life to feed them.
Sometimes I want to keep everything all to myself. But God wants
to use me. He wants to use me to
help even the people I don't like.

*I now
rejoice
in my
sufferings
for you.*
COLOSSIANS 1:24

A Prayer

O Lord, please calm the blizzard of busyness that
has blown up around me. Make me an open door
where others can enter and find Your peace.

My thoughts for Jesus

_____

_____

Going Up!

October 1

Jesus is alive inside of my heart. His love rides the dawn of the bright morning sun. He lifts me up to the mountaintops. I will run down the mountain. I will tell all my friends. I will help lift them up. Now they see Jesus, too.

Jesus took Peter, James, and John. . . up on a high mountain.
MARK 9:2

A Prayer

O Lord, sink my little roots deep into the good ground of Your heart so I can draw up love, joy, peace, and the courage to wait and trust in You.

My thoughts for Jesus

_____

_____

Coming Down

October 2

Yesterday God was so real and so close. Today He seems so far away. It's getting dark. And it's getting cold. But God is still here. He is right here in my heart.

"Have compassion on us and help us."
MARK 9:22

A Prayer

O Lord, please help me. I feel like I've been drifting around in dizzy gray circles waiting to be sucked down the drain. Spring up and bring me life again.

My thoughts for Jesus

_____

_____

Fight!
October 3

Has something come between Jesus and me? That thing will have to go! I will grab it by the arm. I will look it in the eye. I will tell it, "Go away!" I will get down on my knees and ask for God's help. And then I will fight until it's gone!

"This kind can come out by nothing but prayer and fasting."
MARK 9:29

A Prayer

O Jesus, thank You for this beautiful place where I can blossom and bloom and pour out my heart to You. I want to stay here forever and ever.

My thoughts for Jesus

_____

_____

I Am the Clay

October 4

Jesus is molding
and shaping my
heart. At times
His hands are
tender and gentle.
At times He must press and
squeeze and pound. But I will
let Him have His way. He is
making something beautiful.
He is making me.

*. . .called to
be saints.*
1 Corinthians 1:2

A Prayer

Thank You, Jesus, for the wonderful joy that has
flooded my heart so deeply this morning. Let every
new day find me in this very same place with You.

My thoughts for Jesus

_____

_____

An Odd Couple

October 5

I can be neat and clean with each hair right in place, or rumpled and mussed like an unmade bed. God doesn't notice. That is not what matters. He is looking at my heart.

And thus death spread to all men, because all sinned.
ROMANS 5:12

A Prayer

O Jesus, thank You for allowing me to see You in sharp, clear focus today. Fill the whole day with the beauty and peace of Your Holy Spirit.

My thoughts for Jesus

_____

_____

I'd Be Happy To

October 6

I am not perfect. And it's beginning to look like
I never will be! I know what to do. But I still make so many mistakes. I feel like I'm just no good. But God is faithful. I can open up my empty heart. God will fill it. He will fill it with His Son.

When it pleased God. . .to reveal His Son in me. . .
GALATIANS 1:15–16

A Prayer

O Lord, set me free from the fog of worry that makes little problems look big and clouds my vision so that I can hardly see You at all.

My thoughts for Jesus

_____

_____

Be That Way

October 7

When I do something wrong, that is a sin. And God wants me to do the right thing. But He wants me to *be* the right thing even more. Jesus forgives wrong-doing. But He died on a cross so I could be right with Him.

He made Him who knew no sin to be sin for us.
2 CORINTHIANS 5:21

A Prayer

O Lord, I know I've been a lazy, ugly blob of green goop lately. Thank You for touching me and showing me that my only real beauty comes from You.

My thoughts for Jesus

_____

_____

I'm Listening Now

October 8

Am I listening
for God's
voice? Or
am I listening for
my own? I would love
to do big things. And maybe
I will. But is God really shouting,
"Go and do big things"? Or is He
simply whispering, "Come to Me"?

"Come to Me."
MATTHEW 11:28

A Prayer

O Lord, please help me. I am dried up and dusty,
and nothing feels right. Send Your rain to soften
my hardened heart. I want to hear Your voice again.

My thoughts for Jesus

_____

_____

On My Side
October 9

Did I obey God? Did I do what He said even though it was very hard? That's great! But God doesn't want me to be extra good just so people will look at me and think, *Wow! That kid is an angel!* No, God just wants me to stay close to Jesus. When Jesus and I are friends, He will always be on my side. And He will work things out for my good.

. . .instruments of righteousness to God.
ROMANS 6:13

A Prayer

O Lord, here is my heart. Dig in all around me and let the fire of Your Spirit become the wall that protects and the light that guides and guards my life.

My thoughts for Jesus

_____

_____

Suddenly It's Mine

October 10

How can I know
what the Bible
really means?
I can study and
search and think
and be wise and never
understand. But when
I get up and do the
things the Bible says to
do—suddenly it's mine!

*"You have hidden
these things from
the wise. . .and
have revealed
them to babes."*
MATTHEW 11:25

A Prayer

O Lord, please smooth out all my prickles and
stings. I don't want to pinch or poke anyone with
my words anymore. I just want to be like You.

My thoughts for Jesus

_____

_____

Silence

October 11

I prayed. And God heard me. But how do I know? He didn't say anything back. But God knows that I love Him. He knows He can trust me. I can trust Him, too. My heart is quiet. The answer will come.

He stayed two more days in the place where He was. JOHN 11:6

A Prayer

O Jesus, how I long to know You are with me right now. Here is my heart. Light up the silence of this good day with the the warm glow of Your peace.

My thoughts for Jesus

_____

_____

Walk with God

October 12

I want to walk with God. But sometimes it's hard to keep up with Him! He does things so differently than I would. Is Jesus out ahead of me just now? I will run to catch up. I will do this His way. I want to walk with Him.

Enoch walked with God.
GENESIS 5:24

A Prayer

O Lord, I have so much to do. I don't know where to start. Please come into this day in an extra large way. I need You more than words can say.

My thoughts for Jesus

_____

_____

Don't Look Now!

October 13

Where is God? Why doesn't He say anything? I wonder if my dreams will ever come true. I've been waiting so long. But I'm not going to give up now. Maybe God has to change a few things first. Maybe He has to change *me.* Then I can really love Him. And then He can use me to help the people around me.

He went out to his brethren and looked at their burdens.
EXODUS 2:11

A Prayer

Thank You, Jesus, for a heart and mind that are quiet and still. I can sleep in undisturbed peace, for You are always awake and watching over me.

My thoughts for Jesus

_____

_____

Tell Them

October 14

People all over the world need to hear about Jesus. And God wants me to tell them. But first He must be alive inside of my heart. When I grow up, God may send me across the world—or across the street! I will let Him decide. God is not my servant. I am His.

"Go. . . and make disciples of all the nations."
MATTHEW 28:19

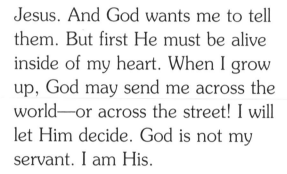

A Prayer

O Lord, please let this little house be so alive with Your goodness and love that everyone who comes inside will be drawn to surrender their heart to You.

My thoughts for Jesus

_____

_____

The Message

October 15

God is good. He is loving and kind. And He has done so much for me. Now I want to tell everyone! But what should I say? Should I talk about these things? Yes! But I must always remember this: God doesn't want people to be exactly like me. He wants them to be exactly like Jesus.

He Himself is the propitiation for our sins.
1 JOHN 2:2

A Prayer

O Lord, thank You for this beautiful morning and for the joy and freedom that are dancing in the clear air of the new life You put inside my heart.

My thoughts for Jesus

_____

_____

Keys, Please
October 16

I want to tell everyone about Jesus. And I would gladly work night and day to do it. But work is not the key to unlock the door to my friend's broken heart. The key to that is prayer!

"Pray the Lord of the harvest to send out laborers into His harvest."
MATTHEW 9:38

A Prayer

Thank You, Jesus, for a quiet heart that hears You say, "I know the plans I have for you, plans to prosper you and not to harm you."

My thoughts for Jesus

_____

_____

Greater Works

October 17

I want to do something great. I want to change the world! But here I am again, stuck right here in the same old place. What can I do today that really matters? What can I do to help? That's easy. I can pray!

"Greater works than these he will do, because I go to My Father."
JOHN 14:12

A Prayer

O Lord, here is my heart. Please come into the middle of this mess and muddle and make something wonderful, real, holy, and new.

My thoughts for Jesus

_____

_____

True Devotion

October 18

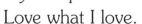

Jesus said, "Do you love Me? Then feed My sheep! Love what I love. Hate what I hate. Trust Me when I've wandered off into the morning mist. Don't worry about things. Just be yourself. And love like I love You."

They went forth for His name's sake.
3 JOHN 7

A Prayer

O Jesus, thank You for teaching me not to worry about whether I'm being useful to You or not, but to simply serve and be a blessing right where I am.

My thoughts for Jesus

_____

_____

Go, Dog, Go!
October 19

Hurry, hurry.
Busy busy.
Big, important
things to do!
No time for this.
No time for that. I can't stop
now. Too much to do! But why?
Jesus is not in a hurry. So I'm
not, either. I think I'll spend
some time with Him.

"My kingdom is not of this world." JOHN 18:36

A Prayer

O Lord, so many things that look like fun are nothing but tools the enemy uses to hurt me. Give me the courage and wisdom to know when to say no.

My thoughts for Jesus

_____

_____

Will I?

October 20

I want to be good. I want to do right. I want to learn how to be loving and kind. I want to let Jesus make His home in my heart. I want to do all of these things. But will I? Jesus will always love me—but only I can decide to let Him change my heart.

This is the will of God, your sanctification.
1 THESSALONIANS 4:3

A Prayer

O Jesus, here is my heart. Draw me so close that Your peace and joy begin to shine out of my life like light shines out of the beautiful summer sun.

My thoughts for Jesus

_____

_____

Walking on the Water

October 21

Peter got out
of the boat.
He walked
across the water!
That was an amazing
miracle. Now Jesus wants
me to do a miracle, too. He
wants me to walk across my
life today in a way that
pleases Him.

*. . .building
yourselves up
on your most
holy faith.*
JUDE 20

A Prayer

O Jesus, I've made a mountain out of my problems
and a molehill of Your power. Show me the way out
of this mess. I want to bring joy to Your heart again.

My thoughts for Jesus

_____

_____

Man Overboard!

October 22

I've been holding on to
my fears and worries as
though they are life jackets to keep
me safe. So why do I still feel scared
and worried? Am I puzzled and confused? God will show me what to do.
But when? When I pack up all my
fears and doubts and fling them all
overboard. Splash! Down they go.
Now there's nothing left to keep me
safe. Nothing but God's Holy Spirit.

*The
Spirit
Himself
bears
witness
with our
spirit.*
ROMANS 8:16

A Prayer

O Lord, thank You for all the good things You have
planned for this new day. Stir up the gift You've
placed in my heart. I am Yours and Yours alone.

My thoughts for Jesus

_____

_____

Not a Bit of It

October 23

Do I hate someone —because of the color of her skin—or the way he talks—or because she acts differently than me? God does not. And He won't let me do it, either. Do I own this secret sin? God will bring it into the light. He wants me to let Him wipe away all my hatred.

If anyone is in Christ, he is a new creation; old things have passed away.
2 CORINTHIANS 5:17

A Prayer

O Lord, please forgive me for making everything so very complicated. Help me to slow down and get back to simply spending time alone with You.

My thoughts for Jesus

_____

_____

Victory!

October 24

I'm fighting to do right. But I'm losing the war! I could struggle and strain to get the victory. But I think I'll run to Jesus instead. He will win the war. I will trust Him. And then I will be a sweet fragrance to Him!

Thanks be to God who always leads us in triumph in Christ.
2 CORINTHIANS 2:14

A Prayer

O Lord, how can You love me so much when I have so little to give? I know I don't deserve it, but here is my heart. Take it and make something beautiful.

My thoughts for Jesus

_____

_____

Here and Now
October 25

Sometimes I think God could use me more if I were older, if I lived somewhere else, if I could do things better. But God wants to use me right now, right here. He wants to be able to say, "This is My child." Here and now, He has a plan that's just for me.

I have become all things to all men, that I might by all means save some.
1 CORINTHIANS 9:22

A Prayer

O Jesus, I'm as stale and dry as a slice of old bread. Please come and soften my heart. Fill this day with the sweet smell of Your warm embrace.

My thoughts for Jesus

_____

_____

Who Is a Missionary?

October 26

A missionary is a person sent by God to teach His Word and share His love. But who is a missionary? That's easy. I am! And who will God send? That's right! He will send me.

"As the Father has sent Me, I also send you."
John 20:21

A Prayer

O Lord, I am so small. And I have made so many mistakes. But You came in and changed my heart. And now I want to tell the whole world about You.

My thoughts for Jesus

_____

_____

Way to Go
October 27

What is the best way to teach the Word of God? What is the best way to share His love? The best way to teach is to know God myself. The best way to share is to live for His love.

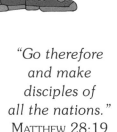

"Go therefore and make disciples of all the nations." MATTHEW 28:19

A Prayer

O Jesus, thank You for opening up Your arms and giving this sack full of worries, mistakes, failures, and sins a safe place to make a brand-new start.

My thoughts for Jesus

_____

_____

It Is Finished

October 28

Why has God
forgiven my sins?
Because I'm sorry? Because
I'm trying to do better? Because
I promise to do what He says
from now on? No. Jesus died
on the cross. And my sins died
there, too! How does it work?
I don't really know. But it is true.
And I do believe it. It is finished—my
sins are already forgiven. I am saved!

Having been reconciled, we shall be saved by His life.
ROMANS 5:10

A Prayer

O Lord, thank You that You are not like a shadow that is here one minute and gone the next. Your love is real and You will never leave me or turn me away.

My thoughts for Jesus

_____

_____

All He Sees
October 29

Why did Jesus have to die? Jesus didn't do anything wrong! But God hung the sin of every person upon Him. When God looked at Jesus on the cross, all He saw was sin. And sin must be killed. So Jesus had to die. But Jesus has risen from the dead. He has risen right here inside of my heart. Now when God looks at me, He does not see my sin. All He sees is His living Son!

. . .that we might become the righteouness of God.
2 CORINTHIANS 5:21

A Prayer

O Lord, thank You for the beautiful new life You give. Help me not to turn to the right or to the left, but to keep moving steadily on toward You.

My thoughts for Jesus

_____

_____

This Is Faith

October 30

Sometimes I feel silly following Jesus. Sometimes I think He asks me to do crazy things. But when I do every little thing for Jesus—no matter how silly— then I can see Him more and more. My faith isn't just in my head now. Now it's in my hands and feet. Now it is real.

Without faith it is impossible to please Him.
HEBREWS 11:6

A Prayer

O Lord, here are my hands. Fill them with strength so I can do Your will. And here is my heart. Your love is only the thing I ever really wanted.

My thoughts for Jesus

_____

_____

Faith Is This
October 31

What will
God give
me when
I learn to
have faith?
What will He
do when I trust
in His Word? God will give
me Himself. He will make me
His own. He will set me free.

*". . .faith as
a mustard
seed."*
MATTHEW 17:20

A Prayer

O Lord, a million bug-eyed little worries are buzzing
around my head today. Come and speak Your peace
so they will be still and I can hear Your voice.

My thoughts for Jesus

_____

_____

Go with the Flow

November 1

Some days
I like to be
all by myself.
But like my
heart, this day
is God's. Will I get to do what
I want to today? Maybe. But
God may have other plans.
So I won't clog them up.
I will go with the flow!

*Do you
not know
that. . .you are
not your own?*
1 CORINTHIANS 6:19

A Prayer

O Lord, draw me back into the secret place. I want
to be with You again. Teach me to be quiet on the
inside so I can hear Your voice clearly today.

My thoughts for Jesus

_____

_____

What to Keep

November 2

Should I do what God says? Should I keep His commands? What a silly question! Of course I should. I love God with all of my heart. Why would I listen to anyone else?

"If you love Me, keep My commandments."
JOHN 14:15

A Prayer

O Jesus, here is my heart. Dig all the way down to the deepest, most unexplored part and read the prayers I am too afraid to pray myself.

My thoughts for Jesus

_____

_____

I Surrender!

November 3

Part of me wants to do God's will. And part of me does not. Is God angry with me for feeling this way? No. Jesus loves me far too much to break in and steal my heart. He is waiting for me to give it to Him.

"I have been crucified with Christ." GALATIANS 2:20

A Prayer

O Jesus, I want to come running to Your side with laughter and joy. But I feel just awful today. Thank You for loving me even when I can't love myself.

My thoughts for Jesus

_____

_____

Do Something

November 4

God is calling me. Now it is up to me to go. I can't just sit here listening. I have to get up and do whatever He says. As soon as I do, He will come and meet me.

Draw near to God and He will draw near to you.
JAMES 4:8

My thoughts for Jesus

_____

_____

Rejoice!

November 5

Why is this happening? What is God doing? I knew just what I wanted. And then, splat! God stepped on it. Just look at it. It's ruined! Now I'll have to want something else. God wants what is best for me.

Rejoice to the extent that you partake of Christ's sufferings.
1 PETER 4:13

A Prayer

O Lord, there's no point in pretending to be good when You know my heart the way You do. Thank You for loving me just the way I am.

My thoughts for Jesus

_____

_____

Believe

November 6

I know what Jesus can do. I know He can heal people who are sick. I know He can feed people who are very hungry. I know He can bring a dead person to life. But can He do this for me? If I believe—He can!

"Do you believe this?"
JOHN 11:26

A Prayer

O Jesus, thank You for breathing new life into this broken body. I am alive again with the joy that comes from the strength only You can give.

My thoughts for Jesus

_____

_____

They Make Me Mad!

November 7

Oh, these people! They make me so mad! Why did God put me here? I'd like to run away! But I must not. God did not put me here to run away! He put me here to pray.

All things work together for good to those who love God.
ROMANS 8:28

A Prayer

Thank You, Lord, for allowing me to come boldly to Your throne to ask for anything that is Your will, knowing You will hear me and answer my prayer.

My thoughts for Jesus

_____

_____

In God's House

November 8

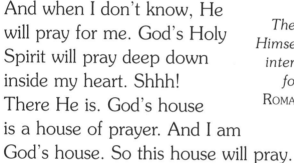

I don't always
know the right
way to pray.
But God knows.
And when I don't know, He
will pray for me. God's Holy
Spirit will pray deep down
inside my heart. Shhh!
There He is. God's house
is a house of prayer. And I am
God's house. So this house will pray.

*The Spirit
Himself makes
intercession
for us.*
ROMANS 8:26

A Prayer

O Lord, let the fire of Your Holy Spirit be the flame
that lights up the lamp of my heart. I want Your
light to burn bright and pure in me today.

My thoughts for Jesus

_____

_____

Lift Him Up

November 9

I want to tell the world about Jesus. But how should I do it? By being cute and funny? By being smart and telling good stories? How silly! Those things make people look at me. And no one will ever find Jesus if they're looking at me. I have to show them Jesus.

I now rejoice in my sufferings for you.
COLOSSIANS 1:24

A Prayer

O Lord, please protect me from the things in this life that would turn my heart and mind away from You. I want to follow You wherever You may go.

My thoughts for Jesus

_____

_____

Come Out and Play
November 10

The weather outside is cold and windy. And it's warm and cozy inside. But God is knocking on the door to my heart. Will I stay inside where it's safe and warm? Or will I put on my boots and go outside and play?

. . .fellow laborer in the gospel of Christ.
1 THESSALONIANS 3:2

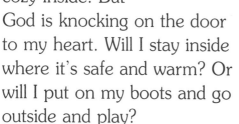

A Prayer

O Jesus, I want to hear Your voice. Teach me to turn away from the darkness all around me so I can glow with the holy light of Your great love.

My thoughts for Jesus

_____

_____

Like Abraham

November 11

Am I happy and content? I will thank God and enjoy His blessings. Is my heart broken and confused? I will trust God and walk alone with Him. He will lead me home.

"Take now your son."
GENESIS 22:2

A Prayer

O Jesus, how I long for You to draw near today. Come squeeze into every pocket and pouch and bring this day alive with the light of Your love.

My thoughts for Jesus

_____

_____

All Things Are New

November 12

Jesus changed my heart. He made every part of me brand new! I don't need to do bad things anymore. I don't even want to. The old me is gone. I am born again.

Old things have passed away; behold, all things have become new.
2 CORINTHIANS 5:17

A Prayer

O Lord, I feel like I'm dreaming. You are so good to me I don't know what to do. How can I ever thank You enough? I want to laugh and sing and jump for joy.

My thoughts for Jesus

_____

_____

Whom Do I Trust?

November 13

Whom do
I trust? I trust
Jesus. Not the
story of Jesus.
And not what
someone has said about
Him. But the real, live
Son of God who took
my sins away. I trust Him.

*. . .the Son of God,
who loved me and
gave Himself for me.*
GALATIANS 2:20

A Prayer

O Jesus, thank You for stepping out of heaven
and walking here with me, right before my very
eyes, in every part of this beautiful new day.

My thoughts for Jesus

_____

_____

Are We There Yet?

November 14

Jesus will lead me. He knows what to do. He will look after everything. Big or small, it's all in His hands. I don't have to ask where we are going. I don't need to know if we're there yet. I can relax and trust in Him.

"As for me, being on the way, the LORD led me."
GENESIS 24:27

A Prayer

Thank You, Lord, for eyes that never fail to see Your beauty and goodness in everything You are and all You have done for me.

My thoughts for Jesus

_____

_____

It Isn't Easy

November 15

Sometimes I want to fix my friend's life. I want to tell him how to act. I want to help Jesus change him. But God wants me to get out of His way. He wants me to look at Jesus and wait for Him. And then Jesus will take care of my friend.

"What is that to you? You follow Me." JOHN 21:22

A Prayer

O Lord, here is my heart. Take the threads of my life and weave them together into a beautiful tapestry of holiness, worship, and praise.

My thoughts for Jesus

_____

_____

Halo There!

November 16

No one may notice me today. No one may say anything about the good things I do. That's okay. I'm not looking for a spotlight. I'm not trying to buy a halo. God knows where I am. That's good enough for me.

Whatever you do, do all to the glory of God.
1 CORINTHIANS 10:31

A Prayer

O Lord, thank You for the courage to banish fear and doubt from my life for good so I can do what You ask with boldness, strength, and joy.

My thoughts for Jesus

_____

_____

I Will Bless You

November 17

When Jesus
says, "Come,"
I will come.
When He says,
"Let go," I will
let go. When He says,
"Trust Me," I will trust
Him. When God speaks,
I will listen. "Now," God
says, "I will bless you!"

"Because you have done this. . .I will bless you."
GENESIS 22:16–17

A Prayer

O Lord, please forgive me for pulling the covers up over my head and going back to sleep when I heard You tell me to get up and get moving.

My thoughts for Jesus

_____

_____

I Can—I Will!

November 18

Jesus will not do everything for me. He wants me to do some things myself. Did He ask me to stop doing that very bad thing? I won't say, "I can't." I can—and I will.

"If the Son makes you free, you shall be free indeed."
JOHN 8:36

A Prayer

O Jesus, please come and pour out a river of living water into the desert of my broken heart. I want to be filled to overflowing with Your goodness and love.

My thoughts for Jesus

_____

_____

He Can—He Will!

November 19

I have sinned. I broke God's heart. How can He ever forgive me now? Sin must be punished! But God did not punish me. He punished Jesus instead. His death was the punishment for my sin. Oh, how God loves me. Now He can forgive me.

When He has come, He will convict the world of sin. JOHN 16:8

A Prayer

O Lord, no matter how hard I try, I just can't seem to do anything right. Teach me to rest and let my roots sink deep into You so I can bear good fruit.

My thoughts for Jesus

_____

_____

I Forgive You

November 20

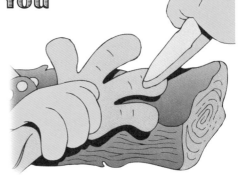

God is love.
He is gentle
and kind. He
has forgiven
all of my sins.
Not because He loved
me, but because Jesus
died. God's forgiveness
cost Him His Son.

*In Him we have. . .the
forgiveness of sins.*
EPHESIANS 1:7

A Prayer

O Jesus, please forgive me. I don't need to be
important. I don't always have to win. Here is
my heart. I just want to be Your child.

My thoughts for Jesus

_____

_____

Come and Get It!

November 21

Jesus hates sin. He hates the terrible thing it does to my heart. He hates how it hangs on and will not let go. He hates it so much that He died to destroy it. And destroy it He did! It is finished. My heart is free.

"I have finished the work which You have given Me to do."
JOHN 17:4

A Prayer

O Jesus, please help me. My heart feels so lonely and You seem so far away. Forgive me for taking so little time to slow down and get closer to You.

My thoughts for Jesus

_____

_____

Off the Deep End

November 22

The ocean is beautiful and deep. But the way to the deepest, most wonderful part begins by getting my feet wet on the shore. I don't understand everything about God. And there's no need to pretend that I do. But I hear His voice. He is calling my name. And step by step He will lead me out into the deep—until at last I'm home with Him.

Whatever you do, do all to the glory of God.

1 CORINTHIANS 10:31

A Prayer

O Lord, come and blow the clear, crisp wind of Your Spirit over my heart today. Spark my sleepy brain back into action and fill this day with Your new life.

My thoughts for Jesus

_____

_____

Wrong, Wrong, Wrong

November 23

My friend is wrong. Wrong, wrong, wrong! Why can't she see it? Why won't she change? I've got to do something. But what should I do? Should I tell her about it? Should I try to set her straight? No! I should pray for her.

Have mercy on us, O LORD.
PSALM 123:3

A Prayer

O Lord, make me so sensitive to Your voice that I can hear the softest whisper. You don't need to send a donkey. I am listening for You.

My thoughts for Jesus

_____

_____

I've Sprung a Leak!

November 24

Help! I've sprung
a leak in my faith!
I'm not sure that God loves me!
I'm not sure I can trust Him! I'm
not sure that He's leading in just
the right way! Oh, look. Here's
the problem. My eyes aren't on
Jesus. But I can fix that! Now
I can see Him. Now my faith's not leaking.
Now He can fill me up right to the top!

*Our eyes
look to the
LORD our
God.*
PSALM 123:2

A Prayer

O Lord, when will I ever learn to allow the new life
You placed in my heart to change my words or my
deeds or the way I treat my family and friends?

My thoughts for Jesus

_____

_____

Deep Roots

November 25

Seasons will change. Friends will come and go. But one thing will always stay the same. Jesus loves me. He set me free. My roots grow strong and deep down into Him.

God forbid that I should boast except in the cross of our Lord Jesus Christ.
GALATIANS 6:14

A Prayer

O Jesus, I feel like I'm drifting alone in the dim light of a never-ending winter. Touch my heart with Your light and make everything beautiful, warm, and new.

My thoughts for Jesus

_____

_____

The Message
November 26

I can tell my
friend about
God's blessings.
I can tell him
all about the good
things God can do. That
is good. And I should tell
him. But it is what Jesus
did on the cross that will
change his heart.

*. . .except in the
cross of our Lord
Jesus Christ.*
GALATIANS 6:14

A Prayer

O Lord, I don't know much. But I do know this:
You took my sins and nailed them to the cross.
And no one can ever take that away from me.

My thoughts for Jesus

_____

_____

In It but Not of It

November 27

Jesus lived in the world. He did not live far away in a place by Himself. The things of this world did not drive Him away from God. Jesus did not come to this world to get things. Jesus came here to get me. He wanted us to be friends.

. . .by whom the world has been crucified to me, and I to the world.
GALATIANS 6:14

A Prayer

O Jesus, thank You for the buoyant breeze of Your Holy Spirit that stirs my heart and lifts my voice into swirling winds of worship and praise.

My thoughts for Jesus

_____

_____

For Rich or for Poor

November 28

I can never earn
God's love.
I won't ever
deserve it—
no matter
what I say
or do. God's love is a gift.
He gives it for free! It can
never be bought. All I have
to do is take it.

*. . .being justified
freely by
His grace.*
ROMANS 3:24

A Prayer

O Lord, I have no gift to give You. And I haven't ever
done anything special or important. But here is my
heart. Please take it and make something beautiful.

My thoughts for Jesus

_____

_____

That Explains It!

November 29

I want to be
a Christian—
a real Christian.
Not just a nice
person who
goes to church a lot. A peron
whose life cannot ever be
explained—except by Jesus.
I want to be such good friends
with Jesus that people will see
Him when they look at me.

"He will glorify Me."
JOHN 16:14

A Prayer

O Lord, please come and roll me out of this cozy
little bed. I want to be Your willing servant, ready to
go anywhere and do anything You want me to do.

My thoughts for Jesus

_____

_____

I Am What I Am

November 30

I am not a saint. Or am I? Sometimes what I really mean is "God can never make a saint out of me!" And God most certainly can. So that is not the question. The question is: Will I let Him?

His grace toward me was not in vain.
1 CORINTHIANS 15:10

A Prayer

O Lord, polish and sharpen the gleaming sword of Your Spirit here inside my heart. Restore its cutting edge that I may reflect Your holy light once more.

My thoughts for Jesus

_____

_____

That Is the Gospel

December 1

Have I broken God's commandments? God is not pleased. I must be punished. That is the law! But Jesus took my place. He said, "Punish Me instead." That is the gospel! The price has been paid to take my sins away. I am not a prisoner of sin anymore. I am free!

For whoever shall keep the whole law. . .
JAMES 2:10

A Prayer

O Lord, fill up the air that surrounds me so completely with Your Spirit that rivers of living water flow out of my heart and into the lives of my friends.

My thoughts for Jesus

_____

_____

Just Right!
December 2

Am I trying to be the perfect Christian? Am I working hard to put on a pretty show? If my heart is set on me, people will be drawn to me. But if I give my heart to Jesus, people will be drawn to Him.

Not that I have already attained, or am already perfected...
PHILIPPIANS 3:12

A Prayer

O Jesus, Your hands already hold everything I will ever need. So here is my heart. Fill it with the kind of treasure that will make me want to be more like You.

My thoughts for Jesus

_____

_____

Getting to Know You

December 3

I want to
share Jesus.
I want my
friends to
know Him, too. But what is
the best way to do it? With
smart words? With fancy
stories? The very best way
to share Jesus with my friends
is to get to know Him myself.

*My speech and
my preaching
were not with
persuasive
words.*
1 CORINTHIANS
2:4

A Prayer

Thank You, Jesus, for the worries and fears that
haunt and harass my heart and mind, for they are
reminding me to slow down and take time to pray.

My thoughts for Jesus

_____

_____

Be Glad

December 4

Jesus said trouble would come. But did He say, "Give up"? No. He said, "Be glad, for I have defeated everything that will ever try to hurt you." And He did! But to do it, Jesus had to fight all the bad things. So I will fight them, too. I will fight to do right. And I will be glad!

"To him who overcomes. . ."
REVELATION 2:7

A Prayer

O Jesus, here is my heart. I want to be like You. Please step out of heaven and into my life and walk with me everywhere I go today.

My thoughts for Jesus

_____

_____

His Temple

December 5

My body is God's temple. Jesus lives here. Do I take care of His temple? Or do I let it see and hear and do things that would break God's heart?

"Only in regard to the throne will I be greater than you."
Genesis 41:40

A Prayer

O Lord, I have allowed the light You put in my heart to become dreary and dim. Please touch me with the fire of Your Spirit. I want to burn bright again.

My thoughts for Jesus

_____

_____

Rainbow

December 6

God made
a promise.
But do I
believe it?
I say, "Do
something, God, and then I will
trust You." God says, "Trust Me,
and then I will do something!"
It's up to me now. Jesus is waiting. Will I give Him my heart?

"I set My rainbow in the cloud."
GENESIS 9:13

A Prayer

O Jesus, I want my life to be everything You ever
wanted it to be. Teach me to settle down
and spread out in the good land You gave me.

My thoughts for Jesus

_____

_____

I'm Sorry

December 7

I have sinned.
I hurt myself.
And I hurt my
friend. But I hurt
Jesus most of all. For it is
against Him and Him only
that I have sinned. Please
forgive me, God. I am
sorry. I want to change.
I want to be like You.

*Godly sorrow
produces
repentance
leading to salvation.*
2 CORINTHIANS 7:10

A Prayer

O Lord, please touch me once again with Your
kindness and beauty. Slow me down. Plug me in.
Charge up my heart with Your power and light.

My thoughts for Jesus

_____

_____

So Deep
December 8

Jesus forgave me! I should not be forgiven. I deserve to be punished. But God forgives me anyway! Because of the cross. Because of His Son. Jesus' death lets God forgive me.

For by one offering He has perfected forever those who are being sanctified.
HEBREWS 10:14

A Prayer

O Lord, a hundred nervous little thoughts start to fly around in my head every time I try to pray. Please help me settle down so I can hear Your voice.

My thoughts for Jesus

_____

_____

It's Only Natural

December 9

It's only natural to want to do the right thing. And there are many good things I can do. But I must never let those good things keep me from doing God's best. Sometimes God wants me to do more than pray. He wants me to do something for Him!

Those who are Christ's have crucified the flesh.
GALATIANS 5:24

A Prayer

O Lord, I want to know You. Help me see beyond all the made-up ideas of who people think You should be and fall down and worship You for who You are.

My thoughts for Jesus

_____

_____

What I Want
December 10

There are
many things
I want. There
are some
I want right
now. But what does God
want? God wants the very
best for me. When I give
God my wants, He will
give me what I need!

*Abraham had
two sons.*
GALATIANS 4:22

A Prayer

O Jesus, how I thank You for blowing so softly into
the hidden corners of this beautiful new day and
spreading life and joy all over everything I see.

My thoughts for Jesus

_____

_____

Delicious!

December 11

My special talents and gifts are like the husk on a delicious ear of corn. They are a wonderful part of me. But they are the outside. To get to the beautiful gold inside, I must let Jesus peel my husk away.

"If anyone desires to come after Me, let him deny himself."
MATTHEW 16:24

A Prayer

O Jesus, how I thank You for the wonderful joy that comes from knowing You are my Daddy and I will always be safe and warm here at home with You.

My thoughts for Jesus

_____

_____

Tip of the Iceberg

December 12

I whisper, "I can't," and God whispers, "You can." I'm alone and afraid. But He whispers, "Fear not," as He leads me into the darkness. What can God see that I cannot? He can see into my heart. He can see Jesus.

". . .that they may be one just as We are one." JOHN 17:22

My thoughts for Jesus

_____

_____

His Place—Her Place

December 13

I want to pray
for her. But where
do I begin? Do
I put myself in her
place? No! Her place is a mess!
I must put myself in God's place.
I can't fix her broken heart. She
can't fix it, either. But God can.
So I will pray. And soon she
will come running home to Him.

Men always ought to pray and not lose heart.
LUKE 18:1

A Prayer

O Jesus, thank You for taking this homeless little
heart and replacing its tired, filthy, worn-out, rags
with the beautiful new coat of Your incredible love.

My thoughts for Jesus

_____

_____

Planting Peace

December 14

Did I do what Jesus asked? Then God's blessing will be peace. Did I do something else? Yes, I have pulled up all God's peace. I planted worry in its place. Now I have to pull up the worry and wait. Soon I will see what God will do next!

"Let not your heart be troubled."
JOHN 14:27

A Prayer

O Jesus, thank You for these wonderful times of prayer that connect our hearts and cause Your beauty to burst into bloom for everyone to see.

My thoughts for Jesus

_____

_____

Good Job
December 15

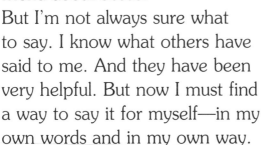

I want to tell my
friend about Jesus.
But I'm not always sure what
to say. I know what others have
said to me. And they have been
very helpful. But now I must find
a way to say it for myself—in my
own words and in my own way.
My friend may not listen to others.
But I know she will listen to me.
So I will not be afraid. I will tell her!

*. . .rightly
dividing
the word
of truth.*
2 TIMOTHY 2:15

A Prayer

O Lord, I want to tell everyone about the good
things You've done. Please put words on my lips
that will unwrap the truth You placed in my heart.

My thoughts for Jesus

_____

_____

Let's Wrestle!

December 16

God wants me to wrestle. But not with Him! I could get hurt! He wants me to wrestle in prayer—to pray and pray until the thing I'm praying for yells, "I give up—you win!"

Take up the whole armor of God. . . praying always.
EPHESIANS 6:13, 18

A Prayer

O Jesus, please forgive me for trying to step into the spotlight and pretend I'm something I am not. If I am strong in any way, it is only because of You.

My thoughts for Jesus

_____

_____

If I Be Lifted Up

December 17

What do
I need?
I need Jesus.
But how do
I know? Because
someone told me! Now
Jesus says, "Tell your friend.
Tell him about Me. Tell him
I died to set him free. Intro-
duce Me to Him."

*But the natural
man does not
receive the things
of the Spirit
of God.*
1 CORINTHIANS 2:14

A Prayer

O Jesus, I want to see You. I want to hear Your voice. I want to soak up Your Word so I can live and grow. You alone are my heart's one desire.

My thoughts for Jesus

_____

_____

This Day
December 18

This day is in God's hands. Tomorrow will be, too. I don't ever have to worry. Things will change. But that's okay. Jesus loves me. I can trust Him. He knows what to do.

All things work together for good to those who love God.
ROMANS 8:28

A Prayer

O Lord, let my heart be fragrant and filled with the sweet song of freedom as we work together to perfume the air with Your goodness and love.

My thoughts for Jesus

_____

_____

Think about It

December 19

She says she is happy
without Jesus. She does not want to
change. That's not so strange. Anyone can be happy without Jesus.
Jesus did not die to make me happy.
Jesus died to make me His. He died
to bring me home. He died to take
away my selfishness and make me full of love.
Sometimes that hurts. Sometimes it doesn't
make me happy at all. But I want to be friends
with Jesus more than I want anything else.

*"I did not
come to bring
peace but
a sword."*
MATTHEW 10:34

A Prayer

Thank You, Jesus, for Your beauty and peace
that calm the wind, soothe the storm, and
soften worry and fear into quiet and rest.

My thoughts for Jesus

_____

_____

One Way

December 20

There are many roads. And each one will lead me somewhere. But will it lead me to God? Whatever road I take, I want it to lead me to Jesus. I don't want to go anywhere else. I want people to see Jesus in my life.

"I, if I am lifted up from the earth, will draw all peoples to Myself."
JOHN 12:32

A Prayer

O Jesus, please forgive me. I have wandered so far away from You. Hide me once again in the stillness of Your secret place. I want to be where You are.

My thoughts for Jesus

_____

_____

I'm Sure!

December 21

Am I sure of myself? Or am I sure of God? God has been so good. Together we have done and seen amazing things. But I must never begin to trust in the things I've done. Those things are good. But they are not my God.

. . .that we might know the things that have been freely given to us by God.
1 CORINTHIANS 2:12

A Prayer

O Jesus, please free me from the prison of my own foolish desires and fill me with Your power, peace, kindness, and love.

My thoughts for Jesus

_____

_____

Here I Come!

December 22

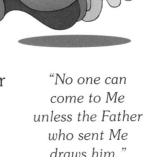

Did Jesus say, "Come"? Then I will come. I won't ask around to see what other people think. Do they know better than God? Of course not. How silly! And neither do I. So look out, Jesus— here I come!

"No one can come to Me unless the Father who sent Me draws him."
JOHN 6:44

A Prayer

O Lord, come and surround me with Your mighty power. Draw up the curtains and let Your beauty flood the secret places of my waiting heart.

My thoughts for Jesus

_____

_____

Good for You

December 23

O Lord,
You're so
good. Your
tender love has
completely changed my heart.
You've made it alive and warm
and new. My old heart is gone!
Now I'm no good for hate. And
I'm useless for sin. The only
thing I'm good for is You.

*God forbid
that I should
boast except
in the cross
of our Lord
Jesus Christ.*
GALATIANS 6:14

A Prayer

O Lord, how I thank You for Your patience and for
the way You are so gently teaching me to come
before Your throne and pour out my heart to You.

My thoughts for Jesus

_____

_____

Hidden with Him
December 24

I am safe.
Jesus is here.
There is room
to live. There
is room to
grow. Doubt
Him? I dare you! Worry?
Just try! I am safe. I am
His. Jesus is here.

*Your life is hidden
with Christ in God.*
COLOSSIANS 3:3

A Prayer

O Jesus, thank You for the joy You've brought into
my life as we walk hand in hand in the secret place
where You can mold and make my willing heart.

My thoughts for Jesus

_____

_____

Happy Birthday!

December 25

Jesus Christ was born into our world on Christmas Day. But where does Jesus live today? Jesus wants to live inside of me—in my heart. When I let Him in, He is born in me, and I am born again!

"Behold, the virgin shall conceive and bear a Son."
ISAIAH 7:14

A Prayer

O Jesus, slow me down and soften my heart. Lift me up into the quiet calm of Your holy light. I want to catch a glimpse of Your beautiful face today.

My thoughts for Jesus

_____

_____

Love Light

December 26

When Jesus died on the cross, He took away all of my sin. Sin moved out and Jesus moved in! Now I just want to be closer and closer to Him.

The blood of Jesus Christ His Son cleanses us from all sin.
1 JOHN 1:7

A Prayer

O Lord, please forgive me. I knew I was wrong. But I jumped right in and did it anyway. Wash away my sin so I can shine with Your holy light once more.

My thoughts for Jesus

_____

_____

What to Do

December 27

God wants me
to trust Him.
I don't always
know the right
thing to do. But
God knows. He will show me.
All I have to do is ask. I can
trust the Word of God. And
when I do, my life will shine
with the light of His love.

"If you will return, O Israel," says the LORD. . .
JEREMIAH 4:1

A Prayer

O Jesus, forgive me for waiting so long. I know it's time to make a change. Here is my heart. Search me with Your holy light. I want to be made new.

My thoughts for Jesus

_____

_____

Made Fresh Daily

December 28

God wants to change my heart. He wants me to be more like Jesus. Is there a part of me that is not like Jesus yet? I will let God change it. Every day I will let God make me a little bit more like Jesus.

"Unless you are converted and become as little children. . ."
MATTHEW 18:3

A Prayer

O Jesus, how I long to see people and things the way You see them. Please lead me out of this darkness and into the clear air of Your holy light.

My thoughts for Jesus

_____

_____

A True Believer
December 29

It's not always easy to do what God asks. The Bible tells me to love and pray for the people who hurt me. I don't always want to do that. But I will do what God tells me to do. He will help me. I will not turn my back on Him. I am a true believer!

Many of His disciples went back.
JOHN 6:66

A Prayer

O Lord, come fill the air with Your beauty and peace. Take my hand. Show me what to do. Please keep me from running headfirst into another foolish mistake.

My thoughts for Jesus

_____

_____

Me, Me, Me, Me!

December 30

God made me special. There is no one else just like me. I can do many things very well, and God loves me just the way I am. But do you know what He loves most of all? He loves to see me becoming more and more like Jesus.

"All my springs are in you."
PSALM 87:7

A Prayer

O Jesus, thank You for the river of new life You put inside my heart. At last I'm flowing clean and clear and fresh and pure. And oh, it's all because of You.

My thoughts for Jesus

_____

_____

Yesterday
December 31

The God of Israel will be your rear guard.
Isaiah 52:12

I know God has good things planned for me in the New Year. But oh my—I made so many mistakes this year! How can Jesus love me when I don't do things right? I just don't know. But Jesus will forgive me. I can't change the things I did yesterday. I will leave yesterday with Jesus. I will walk right out into the New Year. I know Jesus will be with me. He is already waiting for me there!

A Prayer

Thank You, Lord Jesus, for the year that lies ahead. Your hands already hold everything I will ever need. There is no need to be afraid. You will guide my every step. And I will follow You all of my days.

My thoughts for Jesus

_____

_____

INDEX

Bible, the: 1/3, 1/11, 3/10, 4/1, 4/7, 6/5, 6/28, 7/25, 7/27, 9/27, 10/10, 12/27, 12/29

Blessings of God: 2/4, 4/4, 4/9, 11/11, 11/17, 12/14

Busyness: 2/13, 10/19

Caring: 2/2, 2/3, 3/3, 3/30, 7/12

Closeness of God: 5/27, 5/28, 6/25, 7/29, 8/31, 9/5, 10/2, 11/16, 11/25, 12/24

Confusion: 1/12, 1/19, 9/12, 9/14

Creations of God: 1/9, 2/10, 2/11, 5/16

Criticism: 6/17

Desires of God: 1/8, 1/17, 3/8, 3/28, 5/12, 6/2, 6/5, 6/8, 8/19, 9/30, 10/25, 11/5, 12/9, 12/10, 12/27, 12/28

Disobedience: 1/28, 1/29, 2/15, 3/23, 11/19, 12/1

Doing God's Will: 1/1, 1/8, 1/16, 1/29, 1/30, 2/12, 2/26, 3/5, 3/20, 3/26, 4/15, 5/10, 5/13, 5/30, 7/18, 8/25, 8/27, 9/11, 10/8, 10/18, 10/21, 11/2, 11/3, 11/4, 11/10, 11/17, 11/18, 12/5, 12/22, 12/29

Doing Good Things: 1/18, 1/31, 2/5, 2/9, 3/1, 3/13, 3/17, 4/24, 4/27, 5/1, 7/11, 7/17, 7/22, 7/24, 9/9, 10/9, 12/2, 12/9

Doing Things My Way: 1/28, 1/29, 2/28, 5/4, 5/7, 6/27, 11/5, 11/15

Dreams: 2/20, 7/6, 9/23

Eternal Life: 4/12, 5/17, 9/21

Everyday Life: 3/6, 3/22, 5/9, 6/16, 10/17

Faith: 3/28, 4/21, 5/30, 7/29, 8/16, 8/29, 10/30, 10/31, 11/24

Fear: 3/7, 3/15, 4/20, 5/19, 5/24, 5/27, 6/5, 6/14, 8/2, 12/12

Feelings: 1/12, 2/27, 4/16, 5/20

Following God: 1/4, 1/5, 2/5, 2/24, 3/9, 3/15, 3/19, 3/28, 4/29, 6/8, 6/13, 6/16, 7/7, 7/8, 9/14, 9/19, 10/12, 10/30, 11/14, 11/22

Forgiveness from God: 2/18, 2/23, 2/28, 3/21, 4/5, 4/8, 4/20, 5/24, 8/24, 9/8, 10/28, 11/19, 11/20, 12/7, 12/8, 12/31

Forgiveness of Others: 6/22, 6/30, 7/14, 9/25, 9/26

Friendship with God: 1/7, 1/24, 2/8, 3/2, 6/3, 8/4, 8/16, 8/19, 8/21, 8/25, 9/21, 10/9, 11/27, 11/29, 12/19

Frustration: 2/16

Future, the: 1/2, 9/23, 10/14, 12/18

Gifts from God: 1/6, 1/10, 1/22, 2/4, 10/31, 11/28, 12/11

Giving to God: 3/12, 3/13, 3/14, 4/25

Hearing God's Voice: 1/1, 1/13, 1/16, 1/17, 1/30, 2/12, 2/13, 4/7, 5/13, 8/13, 9/10, 9/22, 10/8, 11/4, 11/17, 11/22

Help from God: 2/6, 2/9, 2/16, 2/17, 2/27, 4/13, 5/19, 6/6, 7/5, 9/5, 9/6, 9/17, 10/3, 10/24, 11/6, 12/4, 12/11

Hurts: 2/1, 2/23, 4/14, 5/31, 7/14, 7/30, 9/25

Inviting Jesus into My Heart: 4/11, 6/10, 9/13

Jesus' Death on the Cross: 4/5, 4/6, 4/8, 10/7, 10/28, 10/29, 11/19, 11/21, 12/1, 12/8, 12/26

Knowing God: 3/27, 7/11, 9/10, 10/27, 12/3

Letting God Change Me: 1/12, 3/16, 3/31, 4/3, 4/13, 5/8, 5/12, 5/31, 6/1, 7/1, 7/7, 7/15, 7/21, 7/26, 7/31, 8/14, 8/22, 8/28, 9/8, 9/28, 10/4, 10/13, 10/20, 11/12, 11/30, 12/11, 12/23, 12/28

Loneliness: 1/13, 1/19, 5/22, 7/13, 8/11

Looking for God: 2/14, 3/29, 4/4, 4/7, 6/9, 10/13

Loving Others: 2/3, 2/25, 3/3, 4/24, 5/11, 6/19, 9/20, 10/23, 12/29

Mistakes: 2/18, 3/23, 4/3, 5/24, 6/4, 7/3, 7/31, 10/6, 12/31

Obeying God: 1/11, 7/19, 7/27, 9/9, 9/22, 10/9

Patience: 3/11, 5/2, 5/6, 10/13

Plans of God: 1/17, 3/5, 3/11, 7/28, 8/3, 9/29, 10/25, 11/1, 12/31

Prayer: 1/4, 1/25, 1/30, 2/7, 3/30, 3/31, 4/1, 5/3, 5/25, 5/26, 5/29, 6/20, 6/21, 8/9, 8/24, 8/28, 9/5, 9/16, 10/11, 10/16, 10/17, 11/7, 11/8, 11/23, 12/13, 12/16

Provision from God: 1/26, 1/27, 5/16, 5/21, 6/26, 7/23, 8/6

Seeing Jesus: 4/2, 4/5, 4/8, 6/18, 8/12

Selfishness: 2/23, 4/30, 6/11, 6/12, 6/22, 6/23, 6/24, 7/3

Sharing: 1/6, 5/15, 9/2, 9/3

Sin: 4/10, 6/23, 6/24, 6/29, 9/24, 10/7, 10/23, 10/29, 11/19, 11/21, 12/1, 12/7

Staying Close to God: 4/19, 5/19, 5/22, 8/7, 8/23, 9/10, 10/9, 12/26

Talking with God: 1/3, 1/13, 8/6, 8/20

Telling Others about God's Love: 1/14, 2/1, 2/2, 2/3, 2/15, 2/25, 3/10, 3/17, 3/24, 3/25, 4/24, 5/5, 5/6, 6/28, 7/10, 8/1, 10/1, 10/14, 10/15, 10/16, 10/27, 11/9, 11/26, 12/3, 12/15, 12/17

Temptation: 9/17, 9/18, 9/19

Trusting God: 2/11, 2/22, 2/26, 3/15, 3/28, 4/17, 4/22, 4/26, 5/9, 5/10, 5/20, 5/23, 5/30, 6/14, 8/5, 8/26, 8/29, 9/12, 9/22, 10/11, 11/11, 11/13, 11/14, 11/24, 12/6, 12/18, 12/21, 12/24, 12/27

Worrying: 1/27, 2/7, 4/20, 4/28, 5/18, 5/21, 5/23, 6/2, 6/14, 6/21, 7/4, 7/16, 8/20, 8/26, 9/14, 10/18, 10/22, 12/14